PERSUASIVE
PREACHING

PERSUASIVE PREACHING

RONALD E. SLEETH

HARPER & BROTHERS PUBLISHERS

NEW YORK

Library of Congress catalog card number: 55–8527

CONTENTS

	Preface	vii
I.	The Preacher and His Congregation	9
II.	Persuasion by Character	22
III.	Arousing Interest	33
IV.	Reason as Persuasion	45
V.	Emotion as Persuasion	57
VI.	Dramatizing the Idea	66
VII.	Language of Persuasion	78
VIII.	Delivery as Persuasion	87

PREFACE

THE study of persuasion is a relatively new field. Even though rhetoricians as ancient as Aristotle have considered the persuasive factors of speechmaking, persuasion as a specific field has emerged but recently. Within the past thirty years men like James Winans, C. H. Woolbert, Lew Sarett, and others have formulated the modern theories of persuasion and have given this subject a field-of-study status within the general area of Speech. No doubt it was the advent of the age of mass communication which helped to stimulate this added importance. Now we see persuasion mushrooming into psychology, social psychology, advertising, public opinion, propaganda, semantics, and social control. Wherever human behavior and adaptation to that behavior are considered, persuasion becomes an important factor.

Persuasion is the process of influencing belief and behavior by the use of various appeals in order to win a desired response. The salesman selling a suit, the politician soliciting a vote, the boy asking a girl for a date, the preacher seeking new members for the Church—all of these persons are using aspects of persuasion. And whether or not they are successful often depends upon how well they understand and use persuasion and upon how well the recipients have been motivated to respond in the desired way.

For the preacher, the response he seeks is commitment to the claims of the Gospel. His responsibility is to proclaim this Gospel in such a way that his message meets men where they are and seeks to bring them into a closer relationship with God and man. That is his task as a preacher, for that is the meaning of preaching—to bring God's Good News in Jesus Christ to a needful humanity. An understanding and application of persuasion will help him to achieve this end.

This book, however, does not purport to be a book on persuasion as such. It does not propose to explore all of the area in which persuasion has a claim. The task here is to lift out some of the basic principles of persuasion and apply them to the field of preaching. Nor are these principles original with the author; they are the everyday coinage in any study of persuasion. Any uniqueness this book may possess lies in the application of these principles to the theory of preaching.

It ought to be said, moreover, that neither is this a book on the theory of preaching. There have been so many good books in the realm of preaching theory that another would simply plow over old, even though hallowed, ground. If, however, the preaching of the Gospel can be made more meaningful, more moving, and more alive through the application of persuasive principles, then the purpose of this writer will have been accomplished.

To acknowledge all of my indebtedness would indeed make real Wesley's statement, "The world is my parish." However, there are some men whose names immediately come to mind: Dr. Lewis H. Chrisman, professor of English literature, West Virginia Wesleyan College; Dr. Halford E. Luccock, emeritus professor of preaching, Yale University Divinity School; the late Dr. Lew Sarett, professor of persuasion, School of Speech, Northwestern University.

In the specific preparation of this book, I am indebted especially to Dr. Kenneth Hance, assistant dean, School of Speech, Northwestern University, who read the entire manuscript and made many valuable comments concerning both content and style; to the faculty and students at Garrett who have helped to formulate many of these ideas; and, finally, to my wife, Natalie, whose quiet encouragement was a constant inspiration.

R. E. S.

Evanston, Illinois

CHAPTER 1

THE PREACHER AND

HIS CONGREGATION

MANY people are wary of persuasion; it has questionable connotations. They think of politicians haranguing an audience with empty phrases, or revivalists using cheap sentimentalism to play upon the emotions of their listeners. In light of these extravagances, modern-day preachers are apt to wonder, "Is persuasion crass emotionalism? Is it ethical? How can any speaker, let alone a preacher, appeal to the motives of men in order to manipulate them?"

The answer is not easy, for it is true that Hitlers have used persuasive techniques, and in the field of religion there is an understandable abhorrence of high-pressure salesmanship in relationship to the Gospel. Obviously persuasion can be used for bad ends as well as good. But so can atomic energy, razor blades, and baseball bats. In a free democratic society, persuasion used by various forces competing for a hearing is a check on authoritarianism, and the belief that the combination of the best man with the best cause will ultimately prevail is of the utmost importance to an understanding of persuasion as it is to the workings of a democracy.

Moreover, many of the factors of persuasion are the very factors which help the preacher most effectively to communicate with the audience and there is certainly nothing unethical

9

about good communication. It is merely intelligent preaching to have rapport with the congregation. A church service presupposes a preacher and an audience. The sermon is the point at which the two have immediate contact. It is here that the minister takes up the role of preacher. The preacher who cannot establish a one-ness with his audience is merely verbalizing words and has little reason to expect his congregation to respond with warmth or with action. True, some preachers think that the concern of the preacher in the pulpit should be to raise issues which will lead people into working out their own salvation. Conceded that each man must appropriate the Gospel for himself if it is to be meaningful, still the preacher need not apologize for being an advocate. The preacher needs to raise questions, but if there is any help to be given to men in answering them, with both their minds and their commitments, the responsibility for providing that help devolves upon him. The persuasive preacher is the preacher who lives, thinks, and preaches in the spiritual environment of the needs of his congregation. If the preacher is important to the congregation, the congregation is equally important to the preacher. A wise minister with many years of experience once said to a younger preacher, "Don't count your audience. Look at them. The question of how many are there is not nearly as important as *who* is there."

All during the service the faces of some ministers reveal the number present as accurately as a thermometer records the temperature. If there are 450 present the preacher's expression says, "Oh, what a beautiful morning, everything's going my way." But, if the numbers are down to 325, he wears a worried look. When they go down to 200, he looks as if there was nothing left but suicide.

It would be helpful to remember that Jesus did rather well when he had an audience of only twelve men. One of his greatest discourses was given to one woman at a well in Samaria. He was interested in persons, not numbers. Only when a preacher considers *who* is present on Sunday morning rather than how many he can feel the needs of people and minister to them.

There are several reasons for the preacher's tendency to

forget the individuality of the people in front of him each Sunday morning. For one thing, he thinks of them in this situation as an audience, not as persons. He thinks of the sermon as a speech situation—a situation in which, unfortunately, both the preacher and the people become something totally different in their relationships from what they were before the assembly. For another reason, some preachers feel that the nature of the preached Word makes concern for the listener unimportant. The Word itself is sustaining; if the speaker imparts it he has fulfilled his task. Finally, most preachers simply have not thought about the problem of the audience. Frequently a man does the right thing through common sense, but the field of audience analysis is new and the techniques involved frighten rather than attract some preachers. Whatever the reasons for the neglect of the congregation, it is imperative that the preacher consider those who sit in front of him and the way in which they respond as individuals.

A speaker approaches his audience on a subjective or an objective level, that is, in relation to his own interests or to their needs. The subjective or preacher-interest approach is seen in an incident which occurred in an Anglican parish in England where funds were available for an endowed sermon to be delivered once a year exclusively to charwomen and chambermaids. On one occasion a bright young Oxford graduate was invited to preach. At a high point in his sermon he startled his audience with the rhetorical question, "Some of you are probably saying, 'So much for Cyril of Jerusalem, but what about Theodore of Mopsuestia?'" The story may be apocryphal, but the point is not. Much preaching similarly comes out of the minister's own interests, his own reading, and his own set of mind without regard for the interests of the people in the pews before him. No one would deprecate a preacher's pursuit of his interests, especially his scholarship, because effective preaching is characterized by a unique and individual flavor. Nevertheless, the assumption that whatever the preacher has to say is interesting or important is fallacious. It may not even be helpful to a particular audience. For instance, most preachers experience only failure in trying to preach a children's sermon. Many fail to reach to a youth group because as adults they have not made the necessary effort to understand the problems of young people. Preaching which emanates from the preacher, practically unrelated to the audience, is subjective preaching.

The objective approach, on the other hand, is the preacher's attempt to stand outside himself and see how he can adapt the Gospel to the needs of his congregation. This, of course, does not mean that he adjusts the Gospel to the prejudices of the congregation, but he is concerned to find the best way of making the Gospel relevant to their needs. An extreme example is Dr. Luccock's story of young Theodore Parker who, because there were milkmen in his audience, preached a sermon on "The Temptations of Milkmen." This concern to deal with the daily problems of an audience is imperative, even though the preacher does not cover every profession in his audience with a separate sermon. Nevertheless, speaking to his people's needs takes for granted that the preacher knows the characteristics of his congregation, that he keeps in mind, for instance, that the majority are farmers, or college students, or Midwesterners, or whatever. On a deeper level it means that his pastoral and counseling functions are basic to his preaching for inevitably he needs to carry the problems of his congregation into the study when he prepares his sermons.

An objective approach to a sermon also demands that the preacher keep in mind the purpose of the talk. Occasions largely determine the purpose because they determine the make-up and attitudes of the audience. For a regular church service an analysis of the sermon's purpose will not be needed week by week, but the celebration of some special day—Family Day, Peace Sunday, Thanksgiving—may change the purpose or tone of the entire situation.

The preacher who is a guest in a strange pulpit is under an added necessity of analyzing the composition of the audience in the light of the special occasion. Dedicating a new church is obviously very different from preaching at a funeral. An anniversary occasion is more emotionally charged than is a regular Sunday service. The preacher must be in tune with the occasion. It is obvious common sense that a preacher should not tell jokes at a funeral service, but the common-sense content of sermons is constantly violated. Recently a preacher at a baccalaureate service attended by people from many different faiths and backgrounds gave a violently evangelistic sermon on the faith of his own church—an example either of discourtesy or of a lack of awareness of the purpose and tone of the occasion.

The preacher's own attitude in the pulpit often reflects his approach to preaching. If he is willing to bury his head in a written manuscript, seldom lifting his eyes, and letting his voice fall dead on the vacant row of seats immediately in front of him, he is saying in no uncertain terms that his interest is in himself and what he has prepared to say, not in communicating an urgent idea to the congregation.

An effective speaker needs also to consider certain conditions under which he is to speak, especially if he is a visitor to the pulpit. First, the time allotted for the talk. Congregations, right or wrong, become accustomed to a fairly predictable time devoted to the sermon and grow restless if that time is violated. The small-town church for whom the whistle of the 12:05 passenger train was a more effective terminator than was the preacher's benediction may be an extreme example, but it serves as a reminder that time limits are important. A sermon does not always have to be short, but it does have to be proportioned to the other elements of the service to make a unit of the period set aside for worship and edification.

Also the physical setting for the talk needs to be taken into consideration. How large is the sanctuary? How are the acoustics? Is it necessary to use a public address system? Does the church use any unusual devices during its service? One visiting preacher was disconcerted to find that when it was time for the sermon all of the sanctuary lights were turned out except a large spotlight which made it next to impossible for him to see the congregation or his notes.

Occasionally a man finds himself in a church where the pulpit and lectern are too short for him. If he is a guest speaker he can only make the best of the situation but if the church is one to which he has recently been called, one of his first acts might be to ask the trustees to lift the furniture unto the Lord

—about six or eight inches. Or if the pulpit is too tall for him and it is not adjustable the preacher is excused for mounting a soapbox or reasonable facsimile. There is nothing less persuasive than a preacher peering over the top of the pulpit.

Most pulpits or lecterns are equipped with a pulpit Bible from which the preacher is expected to read the lesson. Although there is something sacrosanct in reading from the pulpit Bible, the roof will probably remain intact if because of poor lighting or poor type or less acceptable version the preacher prefers to carry his own Bible into the pulpit. If he is in a strange pulpit and reads from his own copy he should be sure there is some place to put it after he had read the lesson.

Sometimes a minister in his own pulpit would be more effective in reaching his congregation if he gave attention to the acoustics of the sanctuary, even though it takes weeks of experimentation to find where a drape or a wire will help eliminate an echo. The overly reverberating voice is as difficult to follow as the weak voice. The minister who understands the acoustics of his church can make an effort to accommodate his voice and speed of speech so as to place as little strain as possible on his congregation.

The size of the audience also affects the speaking situation. If inclement weather reduces a normally large crowd to minimal size, the preacher has an entirely different situation from that for which he had prepared. He may well remember the words "where two or three are gathered together in my Name." The sermon may take on an informality and spontaneity which had not been in his preparation for a larger congregation, and lo, the sermon gains in effectiveness.

The characteristics which motivate a congregation furnish important data for the one who is conducting the service. For instance, the predominant age of an audience is an important factor in a successful occasion. Just as youth probably does not care to sing, "Abide with me, fast falls the eventide," so a congregation dominated by older people will scarcely want to "Sound the battle cry." The preacher needs to screen his material in relationship to the age groups within the congregation. He may be losing his young people because his sermons are aimed at adults past middle age. Or his adults may be staying at home because he is overplaying for the attention of the young people. Although every sermon cannot meet the specific needs of every age group, the preacher needs to visualize the way in which the various groups will respond to his material. Recently the age differential in an audience was forcefully demonstrated when a preacher speaking to a college congregation at a summer camp was overwhelmed to find some sixty visiting intermediates sitting in the first few rows.

The predominant sex in an audience is also an important factor. One preacher, invited into a small church as a guest speaker, faced a good-sized congregation, but noted only three men in the group. This fact says something about the church and its witness in the community, but it also admonishes a preacher to take the man-woman balance into account when possible in preparing a sermon. There are psychological differences. Women are said to be more sensitive, more idealistic, more sentimental than men; men more hard bitten, more realistic. Any preacher knows that these generalizations are oversimplifications, yet he also knows that he needs to present his message differently to each group. If he understands the make-up of his audience he will adapt the theme, the illustrations and the emphasis so that he is persuasive in his given situation. Hence, he is also able to preach the Gospel more effectively.

Another important factor in audience analysis is the predominant occupation of the people. A campus church filled with students and faculty calls for a different approach from a small rural congregation, even though one group is not necessarily more thoughtful than the other. A suburban church and one located in a factory area may have equally genuine concern for humanity but they express it in different language and may respond with different projects. Plainly, occupational interests affect audience reaction and level of perception.

It follows that the preacher has to be careful lest he get into the role of special pleader for the ideas and interests of his congregation. There is an equal temptation to steer clear of issues against which his people have a prejudice. A knowledge of the major affiliations of the people in a congregation is valuable in helping a preacher understand the mind slants in his audience. If there are many members of the Grange, or the Farm Bureau, the American Legion, the Masons, these affiliations have helped set attitudes and have a bearing on the way in which the message from the pulpit needs to be presented as well as the response to be expected from it.

The educational background of a congregation also affects their attitudes, interests, and responses. However, the preacher must refrain from generalizing about groups before he knows them. There was a time when it could be assumed that a rural congregation had few college graduates in its midst. Nowadays as a result of increased college enrollments and the movement of urbanites into country homes, many rural congregations have a sizable proportion of college people. A visiting minister in a small rural church, approached after the service by a modestly dressed man, was startled by his question, "Can you explain to me the difference between the existentialism of Sartre and that of Kierkegaard?"

The preacher who takes into account these various factors that help determine a happy relationship between speaker and audience has gone far in establishing good rapport with his congregation. If he pushes his analysis a step further he will discover that congregations fall into three groups according to their predisposition toward speaker, subject material, and response sought.

First, there is what may be called the believing audience, the audience which is kindly disposed toward the central idea and the speaker. There may be disbelievers in the group, but in the main, the audience is sympathetic to the speaker and his point of view. This type of audience is found at anniversary addresses, commemoration occasions, funerals, and generally speaking, in church congregations. If they were not essentially predisposed toward the basic idea of religion they would not be in church. Not all are believers in the usual sense of the word, but they are receptive to some religious thrust from the pulpit. Even the skeptics in a congregation are usually susceptible to the mood which is created in the worship service.

Second, there is the doubting audience, the audience in a state of suspended judgment. A preacher finds such a group when he is facing fellow ministers to discuss the latest word on demythologizing holy writ. An ordinary church congregation may also become at certain times a doubting audience. When the preacher speaks on peace, abstinence, or foreign missions it is entirely possible that he will face a certain number of skeptics and doubters.

Finally, there is the disbelieving or hostile audience. A preacher does not face this audience often. Occasionally in a college chapel where there is compulsory attendance he meets this response, but even here the basic hostility, however expressed, is not toward him.

Before the preacher understands the approach to be made to disbelieving audiences, he must first understand the sources through which people accept belief, so that he can organize his material in such a way as to gain the desired response. People tend to believe through their experiences. Either they perceive for themselves or they draw upon memory, imagination, or reports of others. In religion, the individual's Christian experience is considered basic. The preacher's witness to the experience of the Gospel in his own life, and in the lives of others, is an important aspect of both belief and persuasion.

Beliefs also come through authority. At this point the ethical persuasion of the preacher is relevant. By some preachers the Bible, the Church, the creeds can be used as authoritative, as well as certain secular sources such as the classics or the lives of great men.

People also believe through reasoning. Since the mental processes are important in helping people come to their beliefs, the preacher needs to take special care in his use of logic, evidence, and general supporting material.

Knowing that people believe through experience, authority, and reasoning, the preacher has an idea how to approach the audience after their probable mental attitude has been ascertained. If he surmises that the audience is hostile, for example, probably the best approach is through the authority and character of the speaker himself. Actually an audience is usually more hostile toward an idea than toward a speaker. To cite a case: if the preacher is speaking in opposition to universal military training before a local chapter of the American

Legion, he can be relatively sure of a hostile audience. But even here the members are probably less hostile to the speaker than to the idea he is representing. Therefore, if they accept him as a person of integrity, they will at least open their minds to his idea. In addition to the persuasion resulting from his own integrity he will cite the opinions of experts (authority), facts and evidence (reasoning), and finally utilize material based upon experience.

The speaker who faces a doubting audience finds his primary approach to be through reason, followed by authority of self and of experts with enough experience material to keep the speech interesting.

In the case of the believing audience the task is to intensify mild belief, revitalize a dormant belief, or activate a static belief. Here the preacher may draw heavily upon the materials of experience as recorded in the lives of the saints, of Jesus, of contemporary Christians, and in his own life. Appeals to authority and reason then become secondary.

These categories obviously are not hard and fast, nor all-inclusive. Certainly there is the apathetic audience, utterly indifferent. They fail to react and the problem becomes one of getting attention. A preacher need not be a professional student of audience behavior, but he should have an untiring desire to understand the reactions of his people to his message.

Beyond these general characteristics of audiences, there are other more personal factors which also have to be taken into account. These factors lie more specifically in the realm of psychology, and since persuasion deals with motivation, they must be understood.

Even though the word "persuasion" is sometimes used as synonymous with psychology, or at least with applied or practical psychology, there is no desire here to attempt a full-blown discussion of man's needs and nature according to psychology. Nevertheless, it is helpful to realize that psychology has changed through the years in its understanding of man and his needs. Earlier psychologists approached man through instincts. Later there were the behaviorists, with the emphasis upon stimulus-response and the two important drives of sex and self-preservation. Freud emphasized the sex drive as basic to man's nature; Adler spoke of the drive for superiority or self-esteem. Whatever the development or the labels, each school assumes that there are basic needs within man which motivate him to certain types of behavior. Obviously a speaker must be aware of these needs, whatever they may be called. Most especially should a preacher, whose function it is to minister to the basic needs of man, understand the primary drives.

One of these urges is the drive for self-preservation. This drive is basic, being rooted both in man's psychological and physiological make-up, expressing desire for food and shelter, not only in the elemental sense, but in their social manifestations. Wrongly emphasized this disposition to protect one's interest may make a person crass and mercenary. When too strong it results in the world-owes-me-a-living philosophy. Aware of this need, the preacher through the idealistic approach of the Gospel can reach people and satisfy the need by placing it on a higher level than self-centeredness. For example, he may show that the Gospel provides a warm, inner tranquillity of spirit, a serenity of soul which in turn makes a man more acceptable as a friend and neighbor. He becomes desirable and the result is a desire to preserve this spiritual quality rather than mere physical preservation. Even the appeal to immortality has its thrust at this need.

The basic drive of sex should be understood in its larger manifestations—the desire to love and be loved. What the Gospel has to say to marriage and the family is related to this drive and finds a real response in most people. The sublimation of this drive used creatively may channel power into worth-while fields of endeavor. The widow who transfers her love to humanity and becomes a missionary exemplifies this process. On the highest level, this need is satisfied in the relationship of man to God. The Gospel affirms that God is love and that as children we can have a loving relationship with Him.

Man also feels the need to strengthen his ego, to achieve superiority and thus to win respect and approval of others. This is the drive for self-assertion. This urge, although often frowned upon, has real value. Psychologists tell us that an important aspect of human behavior is learning to love and to respect oneself. The fact that our fatih proclaims that man is "a little lower than the angels" and is "made in God's image" has relevance for the preacher. In the Gospel this self-esteem is the basis of the command "to love thy neighbor as thyself." Like any other basic drive, when it is developed out of proportion to the others it assumes a sinister place in one's life. When the urge is too strong we get close to the basic sin of mankind, for the desire for superiority can curiously become self-idolatry and lead to the very antithesis of the Gospel. The sin of pride can become the most dangerous of all sins, and some would place pride close to the doctrinal concept of original sin.

It takes a wise preacher to understand this drive for ego fulfillment and to present the Gospel accordingly. He may be tempted to root his message on the level of abasement, driving at man's sense of inadequacy. "Repent, ye sinners" becomes his primary slogan. On the other hand, it may be just as disastrous to bolster the egos of the congregation to the place where they feel smug, complacent, and self-satisfied. The intelligent preacher will balance the love-judgment proclamation of the Gospel in his appeal to his people.

Another drive, particularly strong in church members, is altruism. This urge is the desire to serve others, to promote the common good. Missionary giving, help to the poor, and even churchgoing itself may spring from this need, and the preacher should note this drive in his desire to win responses to the Gospel.

Many other needs and drives need to be understood; safety-risk; pugnacity-peacefulness; acquisitiveness-dissipation; curiosity-contentedness. All these urges are buried within those who sit in congregations Sunday after Sunday.

Understanding man's basic needs, the preacher attempts through persuasive preaching to motivate the congregation toward some desired end. He needs to know the congregation as individual persons, to adapt to them, and to present the Gospel in a challenging way to elicit acceptance. All Christian ministers are trying, on the deepest level, to motivate acceptance of the Gospel. Beyond that general good, in any specific sermon they may have in mind specific responses.

"Open your minds," "Think about this matter," "Do something about this idea," or "Come to the altar." Preaching with a goal gives directness and force, but it calls for sensitive understanding of those who sit in the audience from week to week. Such understanding is not too much to ask of the preacher if he is to be persuasive. Yes, if he is to be a good minister of Jesus Christ.

CHAPTER II

PERSUASION BY CHARACTER

IF IT IS necessary for the preacher to be constantly aware of the individuals in his congregations, it is equally essential that he remember they are considering him as an individual also. While laboring to reach his audience with a persuasive message he may forget that one of the most persuasive factors in a sermon is the character of the preacher. Almost anyone would subscribe to the validity of this affirmation. Yet oddly enough, the preacher himself may be so busy concentrating on his subject matter, his preparation, and his delivery that he easily forgets the important part he as a person plays in the effectiveness of his preaching.

The importance of the "call" to the ministry has been emphasized almost universally by writers in the field of homiletics. Everyone will admit that sincerity and a commitment to the Christian Gospel are necessary for the preacher if he is to be able to witness to others. Also, that to be effective the preacher must have experienced some deep spiritual relationship with God. The minister's prayer life, devotions, and Bible study are all important in his preaching. Without strong commitment and a consecrated spirit he can hardly expect to be an effective preacher.

It is not too much to say that the minister as a man is a stronger witness to the Christian message than is the minister as a preacher. Many excellently prepared sermons have failed because the preacher forgot to prepare himself along with the sermon. And many poor sermons have taken on power because a vital relationship with God was revealed by the preacher. This does not mean, of course, that preparation of the sermon is to be depreciated, but only that there is an ineffable quality in preaching which, although due to various factors, is largely determined by the spiritual life of the preacher. Basic to everything he says is his own relationship to man and his fellowship with God. At the same time, there is danger in too much concern with himself, too much introspection on the part of the preacher. He may become too subjective in selecting themes for preaching; he may illustrate himself instead of his ideas; or he may simply be so concerned with his own role that he forgets to be a messenger of God.

The idea that the preacher's character is the greatest factor in persuasion is not a new concept, nor is it necessarily a religious one. The great rhetoricians discovered long ago that the good man, providing his cause is just, will be the most effective in persuading an audience to his cause. It is apparent what this fact means to the preacher. If he is persuaded of his message; if he knows intimately the God who is the source of his message; if this message has changed him and he reflects the change; then he has within his own experience the power, with God's help, to transform others.

The preacher not only needs to see that his personal integrity and character are sound, but he needs to be aware of the way in which his character works upon his sermon, his congregation, and himself. He needs to see the positive or negative reactions which may result from his own person. This is the realm of ethical persuasion.

The importance of ethical persuasion—persuasion arising from the character of the speaker himself—was set forth by Aristotle, who believed that the ethos (character) is the most important aspect of persuading an audience. He even rated ethos higher than the logical aspects of the speech. Although Aristotle mostly limited the importance of character to the speech itself, later thinkers have developed the concept to include events occurring before the speech and functions other than pure composition. According to this view, the preacher is persuading even before he participates in the worship situation on Sunday morning. What he is as a person, a husband, and a friend are all basic to the effectiveness of his message on Sunday morning.

People in a community expect their ministers to set good examples. The average congregation is the first group to admit that preachers are human but—. The "but" is eloquent. It means that people expect the preacher to make the greatest effort to use all his talents of time, money, and ability to the best advantage. True, the day is past when shabbiness was a sign of virtue; congregations like to have their preacher appear well in public—and also the preacher's wife and children. However, when costly clothes are possible only because the merchants carry overdue charge accounts the preacher needs to be wary about talking on the stewardship of money.

The same standard is expected of the preacher's use of time. On moving into a resort area one preacher won instant favor by showing his interest in fishing. But at the end of two years he was in constant disfavor because he was never available for pastoral services. "He's out fishing" became such an established explanation for his absence from the study or the parish that a committee finally suggested to him that the church preferred to enlist the services of a full-time pastor.

A poorly balanced use of time and money through the week, an unneighborly attitude toward neighbors, a poorly organized manse—these and many other practices of a preacher delineate his character so clearly that his Sunday morning sermons cannot erase the picture etched on the minds of his congregation. For the preacher, certainly, persuasion begins at home.

The total of a minister's attitudes, accomplishments, failures, come to a focus when he begins to speak, and positive and negative impressions immediately besiege the minds of his congregation before the sermon begins. Even the personal reputation of a renowned preacher has a vital effect on the receptivity of the hearers. If he is known to be cold and aloof; or shy and diffident; or egotistical or short-tempered—in short, if he is known to be ineffective or incompetent as a person, then his effectiveness as a speaker will be lessened, regardless of the merits of his material.

The newer studies of psychology are a help to the preacher. Increasingly ministerial students are seeing the importance of understanding themselves and their own problems before they attempt to help others. Many of them are taking clinical training, and some are undergoing counseling themselves. Obviously no preacher can expect to exert much influence for good on his people if he shows a lack of understanding of people, including himself. If he has personal problems, then his preaching will reflect that fact. He cannot preach in a vacuum apart from what he really is as a person.

The roles of the minister as preacher and as pastor cannot be separated. If the people discover that he is too busy to call on them or that his calls are overbrief and too business-like, or that he is concentrating on things other than his ministering to people, then he is setting up within their hearts and minds negative aspects of persuasion which will hinder him as a preacher.

Occasionally one still hears the old bromide, "He is not much of a pastor, but he is surely a good preacher." Or a preacher himself may say, "I concentrate on my preaching and let someone else handle the calling." This is a fallacious separation of responsibility. Actually it is doubtful if a person can be a good preacher and not be a good pastor. The farther away from his people the preacher moves (even though it may be to find a refuge to write "great" sermons) the less effective become the sermons. How can he preach to people understandingly if he does not retain his role as shepherd, or if he moves away from his basic material? He may, of course, give great orations or dazzle his audience with verbal pyrotechnics without visiting in his parish, but it is doubtful that he can be effective or persuasive unless he maintains the pastor-preacher-people relationship.

A story is told concerning one of the really great American preachers, Ernest Fremont Tittle. He was well known for his unpopular stands in a wealthy, conservative area. Yet what many people did not know was that this man had the heart of the shepherd, and time after time he stood beside his people when they were in dire need. One man tells of having his preacher walk beside him all night when his wife died, saying nothing, but always there. The man goes on to report, "After that, Ernest Tittle can say anything he likes to me on Sunday morning and I'll take it." When a preacher has been an effective pastor, he has moved far in persuasion; his people are set for a favorable response.

The preacher as a counselor faces the same necessity for close rapport with his people. If he is cold and dispassionate he will not draw men to him; or if he is too talkative he will not actually hear their problems. Many preachers drive people away because they are too easily shocked, or condemn too quickly. A counselor of this type will soon find he is not being sought out for real help. If this estrangement occurs, people will not take his preaching too seriously, particularly when he attempts to discuss personal problems from the pulpit.

Hostility also repels. A preacher may constantly scold his congregation or show a kind of disdain for them. His sermon material becomes subject-centered rather than audience-centered, so that although he is talking to them, they feel left out. In such case, people are hardly drawn to their preacher to discuss some personal problem.

Happily, the preacher who is positive in his counseling, who is wise and considerate, has already persuaded the people to himself so that when he gets up to preach they hear him gladly. Conversely, a preacher in his pulpit may radiate such love and understanding, warmth and concern, that the people respond, saying, "I will hear more of this man—perhaps in his study." What the preacher is as a counselor determines in part his effectiveness as a preacher, and vice versa.

In his role as administrator the personal qualities of the preacher are just as important as in shepherding and counseling his people. If he considers the church peculiarly his church; if he believes it is his responsibility to keep the "machinery of the hierarchy oiled"; if he feels that as the head of the organization he must make all appointments; if he runs the board meetings and keeps final decisions in his own hands; then the people will read the same kind of authoritarianism into his preaching and will react negatively to what he says.

But if he has an understanding of leadership; if he keeps

in mind that he is part of an organism rather than an organization; if he understands and respects differences in personality; if he seeks to lead democratically; if he decides to work with people rather than to work them; then he sets up a favorable response to his preaching.

In short, the sermon does not begin when the preacher stands up at 11:30 A.M. on Sunday morning. If his rapport with the people is good, he has already created a receptive attitude toward the sermon. The factor of ethical persuasion is already at work.

The actual sermon situation in the church service focuses attention on the preacher's character in several ways. Initially character is indicated by the selection of subject or theme. The preacher marked by awareness that the Gospel is relevant to human needs is likely also to be aware that the needs of the specific people in front of him are his first concern. An effective speaker will not speak to a group of mountaineers on traffic conditions in New York City, nor will the persuasive preacher build a sermon on the architectural structure of Solomon's temple.

However, the preacher may be wise in the choice of a subject but still be completely subjective in its development. The latest book in theology may excite him to preach a series of sermons on subjects of peculiar interest to himself. Or he may play on themes of interest to himself—peace, temperance, psychology—to the neglect of other melodies in the score of the Gospel.

At the other extreme, the preacher may be overly objective. After analyzing the congregation which he faces Sunday after Sunday he may yield to the temptation to say what he thinks the people want him to say. To preach Bible-centered sermons because the congregation is reactionary in its social ethics, to preach psychological therapeutics because the congregation considers the Bible outmoded—either extreme indicates a preacher swayed by a desire for popularity rather than devotion to the whole Gospel.

Stated more bluntly, what a preacher does not preach about is an indication of his character as much as what he includes in his sermon topics. A fairly conservative preacher was greeted one Sunday morning by an active member of the League of Women Voters, a young woman equally active in church affairs. "Why don't you give us a good sermon on the Christian as a citizen?" she asked eagerly. Replied the preacher, "I'm not sure the pulpit is the place for such a discussion." "Heavens!" came back her surprised reply, "it's a lot harder to be a Christian citizen than it is to read the Bible every day." What the young woman did not know was that the preacher had stopped preaching from Amos, and then from Jeremiah, and then from Micah. Over a period of years he had narrowed his preaching to comfortable words that shook neither himself nor his congregation out of their complacency. His church was paying the price for his spinelessness by losing the interest of its young professional and business men and women.

Again, a preacher may be varied in his subjects but vague in all his ideas. This formlessness may be the result of poor preparation or an inability or unwillingness to follow a line of thought to its logical conclusion. In any case the people will leave the church confused, their preacher having failed to persuade them of the truth of his message.

A second area in sermon building which reveals the character or competence of the preacher and influences his persuasion is the use of source materials. For example, his source may be the Bible to the exclusion of everything else; or the complete exclusion of the Bible; or nothing but literature; or always illustrations from life situations. Practically any combination of neglect or overemphasis in choice of sources is likely to detract from his competence in the minds of his hearers. The preacher who uses all of these sources in balance not only shows that he can adapt to different levels and interests in the congregation, but probably commends himself to the congregation as a competent and effective sermonizer.

The same might be said for his use of support materials. Often a preacher makes blatant generalizations and denunciations without proof. Some preachers make ex-cathedra statements and then quote Biblical verses to support them—a practice more common in an early day. This kind of unrelated quotation, not supported on other than scriptural levels, is seldom effective in persuading a congregation. Or a preacher may set up straw men and knock them over with relish but without fair treatment.

Amos was a great preacher. He was powerful because he knew how to use supporting material. His central theme was the judgment of God against Damascus, then against Tyre, Edom, Moab. The Israelites being persuaded of the righteousness of God's judgments could only smart under the sting of Amos' words, "Hear this word that Jehovah hath spoken against you, O children of Israel."

A congregation may not like to be convicted of sin but they accept the rightness of the accusation if the preacher has the strength of character to present it squarely. Gaining this acceptance is the first step in persuasion.

One of the qualities which has made Harry Emerson Fosdick a great preacher is the care with which he deals with the various aspects of the problems about which he preaches. His people feel that he is treating the opposition fairly and that he is absolutely honest in making his case. When a preacher shows this kind of competence and care in building his sermon, he is also building a favorable impression in the congregation toward himself and toward his message.

Even in the arrangement of his sermon the preacher's character and competence are revealed. If his outline and development are confused, if the sermon has poor balance, he is revealing adverse ethical persuasion. Some preachers believe it is fashionable to conceal their outline. Although a clear outline may seem pedantic, it is probably better for it to be apparent than to be nonexistent. The saints in heaven and in the congregation rejoice when occasionally the preacher says, "First of all," "Now, in the second place," and "Finally." Rather than boring the audience, a preacher may find relief emanating from the congregation when he helps them to know where he is going and how far he has gone.

Style of speaking reveals a preacher's character. If he believes strongly in the message he is presenting he will want it stated in the most appropriate language. Correct use of the English language is a basic enough necessity that the preacher who has not acquired this skill writes himself off as a mentally undisciplined individual. This requirement does not in the least suggest that a preacher gauge his language to suit a supersensitive English teacher who counts his split infinitives. But it does demand that he use good grammar, choose words for their colorfulness, their concreteness, and their accurate delineation of an idea. For some preachers this precision means the hard discipline of writing out their messages, but this task is not too much to ask if not only a man's character but his message is at stake.

The preacher's character is related to persuasion in his bearing in the pulpit. From the time he appears in the sanctuary until he concludes the service he is saying something to the congregation. If he is careless in conducting worship, if he reads the scripture poorly, if he mangles his prayers, the people will react negatively to his preaching. If he sits slouched behind the pulpit with an indifferent or disdainful eye toward his congregation, he is already "saying" things he probably does not wish to say. If when he finishes speaking he has the air of "I'm glad this ordeal is over," his feelings are sure to be detected and decried. Equally true, if a preacher is at ease on his feet, walks with confidence, and stands with poise, he is setting up positive responses in the minds of his hearers. These factors of competence, along with those of his character and good will, make up this important category of ethical persuasion.

One other important aspect of the preacher's activity in the pulpit which greatly affects his reception by the congregation is his use of direct first-person statements. He may have an "I" complex and speak of himself continually, adding personal illustrations one upon another, and in general dramatizing himself. The preacher who does this is not only undermining the Gospel, but is likely to precipitate a negative reaction. For a while his people may be impressed, particularly if they otherwise love him, but after a time they tire of egocentric preaching. Of course, he need not avoid the word "I" circuitously. Some preachers get themselves tangled into knots in an endeavor to avoid the first person singular, substituting stilted phrases such as "One believes" or "One says." Or worse still, the preacher who refers to himself as "we." No sacred

statute is smashed if the preacher refers to himself as "I."
The only plea is for him to use discretion, lest the congregation unconsciously substitute the minister for the Master,
or tire of the self-adulation.

Equally important is the preacher's attitude toward others.
If he attacks certain persons from the pulpit, he may find
that his congregation feels that he is intolerant of those who
hold views differing from his, and thus lose confidence in him
in his role as pastor. Actually, the preacher who attacks others
from the pulpit usually does so to put himself in a better
position. Whatever the cause, the preacher who deals in
personalities usually reveals his own personality in an un-
favorable light.

The overuse of self in the pulpit is a half-brother to the
equally distressing problem of the dogmatic attitude. Dogma-
tism may result from an "I" complex, or it may come from the
preacher's basic nature, his view of religion, his view of
preaching, or from any number of causes. Not only in what
he says, but in the way he says it, the congregation gets the
idea that thunder is coming from Mt. Sinai. The preacher
needs constantly to remember that he is only a transmitter
of the Gospel and not the Gospel. His attitude should be warm
and friendly. He is a shepherd leading, not a mule driver
standing behind, cracking a whip.

There is a difference between speaking as an authoritarian
and speaking with authority. In the former instance the
preacher may have a tightly knit set of beliefs coupled with
a "Thus saith the Lord" attitude. Obviously, this attitude will
ultimately repel his congregation. Yet his commitment to
the Gospel itself certainly underlies his authority. Jesus was
described as one who spoke with authority. The authority
rested in the nature of his message, but no less in his attitude
when proclaiming it. His straightforward "Judge not that ye
be not judged," was as dogmatic in wording as were the
authoritarian pronouncements of the scribes. But what a
difference!

So it is with the preacher. He does not have to state
dogmatically a narrow view of the Christian faith to which all
must be in accord. He can, however, witness to the fact that

he has known in whom he believes and what God has done for him and others. He can proclaim his experience with all the enthusiasm he can muster without fear that he is being dogmatic.

Fear of positive expression develops in a preacher a disease known as "tentativitis." The preacher is so careful not to embarrass anyone that he repeatedly excuses himself for venturing an idea or even standing in the pulpit. The Reverend Mr. Milquetoast, who in an endeavor to be irenic succeeds only in being dull, is considered by his congregation a man with no convictions. This preacher suggests in a mild, hesitating manner, "I think we might say that 'God was in Christ reconciling himself' . . . so it seems to me."

The attitude which the preacher radiates from the pulpit is an indication of his adequateness. The total impact of character, competence, and good will cannot be overemphasized. The preacher who has a healthy attitude toward himself and others, providing he also has a message, is the preacher who is persuasive.

CHAPTER III

AROUSING INTEREST

WILLIAM JAMES has some wise words for the preacher which should be inscribed on every study wall in Christendom: "What holds attention tends to determine action." This truth is recognized by every effective short-story writer. Pick up several good modern short stories. How many begin with page-long descriptions of the rolling hillsides? None. The action usually begins at once. If it is a mystery story, chances are that a body falls out of a closet within the first two paragraphs. The writer throws out a hook on which to catch the reader's attention. The same should be true for the speaker, whether on platform or in pulpit.

A preacher tends to forget the importance of kindling interest in the sermon. Partly because he faces the same group each Sunday, he assumes he can begin a sermon with the same interest he ended on seven days previously. Often he assumes that because people are in church he can begin to talk about religion at any point and they will listen. Or perhaps he feels, heaven forbid, that he knows what is best for them. Therefore, he begins a sermon as if his people's tongues were hanging out to hear about the Babylonian captivity or about the nature of the Trinity. Now possibly they may be vitally concerned with both of these issues, but usually their attention and interest have first to be arrested.

Most often the preacher fails to get attention simply because he has never thought about the importance of getting attention. Of course, people come into church to worship God, but they come as many individuals with many different things on their minds. They are filled with the cares and worries of the week, and each individual is concerned with the particular problems facing him. Here is Henry Barbour whose wife died of cancer not long ago leaving him with two teen-age children. There is Mary Johnson, in her late twenties, who has just seen an eight-year-old romance end with her fiancé marrying someone else. Here are the Gregors. Their only son is flying experimental, super-jet airplanes for the Air Force. Before the preacher can speak effectively to the needs of a group of individuals he must focus their minds on the theme for the day—a theme which should be vital to them. In order to do this, he has to weld the congregation into a "psychological crowd" and then arouse their interest in the sermon subject. This procedure is not only necessary to determine action on the part of the congregation; it is just as essential to guarantee basic communication.

The worship service precedes the sermon, but how many preachers have thought of the worship service as part of the process of persuasion? Not that worship is designed primarily to persuade, but it does help weld the congregation into a receptive unit as well as lead them into the presence of the Almighty. In fact, if the purpose of worship is to bring together men's hearts and minds for the adoration of God, then a subsidiary value is that the people are united "psychologically," ready to have their interests aroused.

Consider the average worship service. In most churches, the people sing together, pray together, read together, get up together, sit down together. These functions tend to unify them, as indeed all effective worship does. But these functions are also important in relation to the preaching of the sermon. When it comes time for the sermon the congregation should have a feeling of unity, their hearts and minds eager for the message. The effective preacher is concerned with maintaining the unity and the interest already established. That is why he needs to scrutinize his order of service with these objectives in mind.

He may discover that he has the anthem immediately preceding the sermon. From the point of view of getting attention such program building is one of the deadly sins. During the anthem the audience may lapse into subjective wanderings of mind. Certainly they are not actively participating, and that means the preacher will have to work twice as hard at the beginning of the sermon to rekindle their interest and focus their attention on the sermon. If the anthem is effective, possibly ending in a large, major crescendo, the preacher may find himself handicapped by having to start on an anticlimactic level. The situation is comparable to being asked to say a few words immediately after an effective speaker has delivered a tremendous oration. To sustain the interest developed during the worship service and to keep the congregation unified, it would be much better to have the people do something together just before the sermon—perhaps stand up and sing a hymn. In one church, while the congregation is singing the first stanza of a hymn the ushers open the windows, winter or summer. During the singing of the last stanza the windows are closed. The ushers need to work unobtrusively or the exercise may have the effect of preparation for a calisthenics class, but such a practice should help the most soporific preacher.

Even the seating of the congregation is important in getting the attention of a group and then maintaining their interest. A chaplain was guest speaker at a college chapel, an enormous, barnlike structure in which the relatively small congregation was bunched in the middle sections, about halfway back, with two or three individuals sitting separately out in left and right fields respectively. Although the chaplain preached an excellent sermon, it was exceedingly difficult for him to maintain rapport with the congregation. Several things were working against him. For one thing, he was speaking across a chasm, even greater than most preachers face on Sunday mornings. Therefore, although he had good voice, he had to use a loud speaker. Also, the brethren out on the edges distracted the speaker's attention and he was constantly trying to bring them into a unity with the others. They, on the other hand, were mere spectators and never quite felt a part of the group. Such a situation can often be remedied to help the preacher immeasurably and to increase the worshipfulness of the congregation. In this instance, it might have been well to block off one-third of the seats in the rear and to have ushers standing in the center aisle about one-third down to seat the people. This suggestion may be easier to carry out with a college group than with a regular congregation, because most students have not developed vested interests in certain pews in the church. Or, the person in charge might have suggested to some of the chapel committee that they come forward and space themselves in the first few rows, thus encouraging others to come forward when they entered the chapel. Then the congregation, however small, would have been grouped together and close to the preacher.

Perhaps a warning flag should be raised. Although it is the preacher's responsibility to build an effective worship service, the moment he rubs his hands together and smilingly thinks up ways to contrive his audience into a good position he may give the effect of being a master chess player. People resent being pawns although they are willing to be co-operative individuals. It is good to be dramatic, in the proper sense of the word, but theatrics need to be avoided. Bright spotlights on the pulpit, rose petals in the baptismal font, lights of varying intensity throughout the service, except for common-sense necessity—such practices get the preacher treacherously near the brink of becoming a Reverend Mr. Barrymore. The church is a place for worship.

Dignity, however, does not mean dullness. For this attribute in a preacher there is no excuse. He has every right to make his material not only interesting but exciting. After all, the Gospel is the greatest story in the world and it should be respected for its intrinsic interest. It is not by chance that the Bible is the best-loved book in the world as well as the most powerful dynamite in men's souls. A preacher needs give close attention to the way he uses this material in the pulpit.

It is heartening to see a skillful preacher take an old theme and come at it in a new way. He may bring Amos to stand at the corner of Fifth Avenue and Market Street, and scold America for pride of nationalism, or goad individual Americans for bigotry. The prodigal son in modern dress can be found in almost any congregation, and this twentieth-century prodigal, too, may arise and go to the Father. The good Samaritan? What community does not have needs which are being by-passed by the priests and the Levites? These stories are interesting in themselves because they meet real needs, but they can also be treated in such a way that they literally leap from the pages of the Bible and capture the attention of the congregation. Ministers who have specialized in "life-situation" sermons have recently rediscovered the Bible in preaching, partly because it can be made interesting to the modern-day congregation. Because the Bible deals with the great themes of life and death, temptation and victory, sin and salvation, the preacher who can present these themes interestingly and with relevance finds a ready hearing. Job still speaks a necessary word for those who face the problem of evil and suffering; Nehemiah can inspire even the most lackadaisical layman; Moses will strenghten anyone who wavers in the face of great responsibilities.

In an effort to be fresh and interesting the preacher is often tempted to become bizarre. He may treat the Bible as if it were a book out of which to wrench trick texts. The *reductio ad absurdum* is the talk on physical fitness given by a Y.M.C.A. secretary to a group of tennis players. The text was, "And Joseph served in Pharoah's court." The preacher is justified in finding themes that are striking and effective but he may never offend the Gospel or good taste.

In a preaching class a group of students were discussing freshness of approach, and specifically noting the various ways in which the prodigal son story could be preached. It was pointed out that the parable was most often treated in connection with the prodigal himself, with emphasis upon the dangers of riotous living. Then it was suggested that the role of the elder brother might be more apt for the modern congregation, for he was smug, complacent, indifferent, unforgiving. Finally it was pointed out that the real reason for the parable was to illustrate the forgiving nature and love of the Father. One student then suggested that perhaps sometime he would present the parable from the point of view of the fatted calf. There have been themes on no higher level. There is a difference between treating a great theme in an interesting way and drumming up interest for its own sake, resulting in either trivia or jocularity, neither of which presents the meaning of the Gospel.

Having decided upon a theme of interest, the preacher faces the important problem of an introduction to his sermon. Many sermons fail at this point because the preacher does not keep in mind the multiple purpose of an introduction.

For one thing, the introduction ought to disclose and clarify the subject under consideration. This seems obvious enough, but many introductions do not give the audience the foggiest notion of the theme of the sermon. A student minister preached a sermon in which the introduction arrested attention, had good narrative qualities, and was well-delivered. Just one thing was wrong. The introduction had nothing to do with the subject under discussion. When the student was asked about it, he replied, "I know, but it was such a good beginning that I just couldn't resist it."

One way to tie the sermon together is to reveal the problem in the introduction. Thus a sermon on fear may begin by describing the climate of fear in politics, in national affairs, and among individuals. The introduction may conclude with the question, "What does the Christian Gospel have to say about 'fear'?" The body of the sermon would be devoted to answering that question.

Another approach is to let the introduction give the thesis or solution of the entire sermon. A well-knit sermon entitled "3-Dimensional Christianity" illustrates this method.

Perhaps all of you have had the experience of going to the movies and dodging tomahawks, spears, knives, and the sundry items that are thrown out in lieu of a plot. Whatever the drawbacks of 3-dimensional movies, however, they are an advancement in one particular area—they give us a new perspective; an added dimension. Should this same progress not be made in all of life?

We are constantly in need of getting new perspectives in all fields of endeavors; and even as Christians we need continually to consider our faith in terms of new dimensions. *I would like to suggest that Christianity is a faith which has three important dimensions: the past, the present, and the future. And that when any one of these dimensions is neglected or overemphasized, then our faith is thrown out of balance.*

The thesis of the sermon is in italics, and the body of the sermon was devoted to an elaboration of the three points: the past, the present, and the future aspects of faith.

Occasionally, the preacher may want to use a suspense approach in his sermon as a change of pace. In this approach the theme is withheld until the end of the sermon. A sermon on a controversial issue often follows this pattern. However, by and large, the congregation do not come to church to play mental gymnastics with the preacher, and in the introduction they should have an idea of the direction in which the sermon will move.

An attention-arresting introduction may begin with a striking statement. Suppose a preacher were preaching on the plight of the world's peoples and what the Christians can do to solve the problem. "One-half the population of the world is going to bed hungry tonight" is a statement which should catch the attention of the congregation. It should be pointed out, however, that there is a difference between striking and shocking. A visiting chapel speaker once began a sermon by shouting, "I give the Lord thirty seconds to strike me dead." After a long pause he continued, "With these words Robert Ingersoll once began a lecture." It was obvious that the preacher was using this beginning merely for effect; and since his succeeding remarks failed to lead anywhere it was as if a cannon had gone off and a pea rolled out of the barrel.

A striking quotation is another effective way to begin a talk. A sermon on the sense of futility of our age might well begin with the lines of T. S. Eliot:[1]

> Their only monument the asphalt road
> And a thousand lost golf balls.

The use of poetry prompts two cautions. Appropriate lines need to be culled from long quotations. It is possible that a poem of several stanzas will be used on occasion, but only if each stanza is integrally related to the thought being developed; otherwise any extra verses can be purged in favor of the few lines which are pertinent. Also, if at all possible, poetry should be quoted, not read. Especially at the beginning

[1] T. S. Eliot, *The Rock*, New York, Harcourt, London, Faber. Used by permission.

of a sermon, when the preacher is establishing his connection with the listeners, nothing should come between them. It is exceedingly important to begin a sermon by looking directly at the people, and this necessity in itself should force a preacher to pare down quoted material to the amount he can memorize and then deliver it while looking at the congregation.

A different approach is to begin a sermon with a series of questions. "What does it mean to be saved?" might open up a sermon on salvation. Or a series: "Do you know what it means to feel rejected? Have you ever felt completely alone? Have you ever felt lost in a great city?" The theme of loneliness would be thus briefly introduced. Beginning with a question has some marked advantages. If the questions are directly related to the theme, the preacher is forced to answer them before the sermon is finished. Also, effective questions will reflect and anticipate the congregation's thinking and therefore allow the preacher to enter at once into rapport with his audience.

However, too many questions can sometimes backfire, causing the minds of the congregation to scatter in many directions. Questions may also raise more rabbits than the preacher will be able to shoot in one sermon. Still, if the questions are well pointed to the theme under discussion they can be useful devices by which to arrest attention.

The experience approach is another way to begin a sermon. People usually prick up their ears when the preacher refers to some story that has been carried in the newspapers, on the radio, or on television. Or perhaps at times some experience of the congregation itself will be a starting point. Here a knowledge of the predominant interests of his congregation comes to the aid of the preacher. A rural experience, or a school situation, a factory or a business experience—each has a special appeal to a particular group as well as the general appeal of a life-situation story.

Sometimes the preacher may begin with dialogue. Nothing is more effective than a dramatic incident which has a lifelike flesh-and-blood quality. The sermon comes alive with real personalities. A sermon on "The Courage of Christian Witnessing" might begin:

The scene: Paul, a lonely man in chains standing before Festus and King Agrippa. Agrippa speaks: "You have permission to speak for yourself."

"I think myself fortunate that it is before you, King Agrippa, I am to make my defense. Although long a Pharisee, I saw a light from heaven and I was not disobedient to this heavenly vision."

After Paul's defense, Agrippa says slowly, "In a short time you think to make me a Christian."

Although the dialogue has the advantage of making personalities come alive, the preacher should be careful that he does not begin acting out the parts, distracting the congregation, and thus detracting from the message of the story.

Similar to the use of dialogue is the use of narration. The average sermon too often begins prosaically:

This morning I would like to consider the subject of salvation . . . No subject within the Christian faith is of more importance . . . There is no subject about which there is so much confusion . . . It is impossible to be a Christian without an understanding of the change supposedly wrought when we are saved . . .

Such an introduction never gets off the ground. There is nothing in it to catch the imagination. Granted that people may be basically interested in the subject, they can seldom have their interests raised unless there is a beginning which ignites their minds. A possible way to introduce the same subject might be:

One day in a subway, I was approached by a man who handed me a tract and then asked, "Are you saved, brother?" As a minister I was naturally taken aback and for some moments could not answer. What would you say to that question? Some might reply, "Saved from what?" or "Saved to what?" Now these questions are not irrelevant and neither was the evangelist on the subway. For in reality these questions are at the foundation of a man's life.

Again a sermon on the nature of God might begin:

It is reported that a Sunday School teacher once asked her class what they thought of when God was mentioned. One bright lad immediately replied, "When I think of God, I think of an oblong blur." This reply, which has become a classic, might sum up for most of us our conception of God . . .

The narrative approach has the twofold result of getting attention and relating the introductory material to what will follow. All things being equal, the most effective introduction is one which begins with a narrative. Just as a child's eyes open with wild anticipation when a story begins "Once upon a time," the same thing is true for even the most mature congregation. If a preacher can use a story that is interesting and yet pertinent to the sermon itself, he is close to the Kingdom in the matter of introductions.

Frequently a Biblical beginning can be used with excellent results if the principles of good narration are followed. Granted that most introductions should have a twentieth-century setting, still a skilled preacher can arrest the attention of the congregation with a good Biblical introduction. The all too typical approach is:

> In the Gospels we read that Jesus chased the money-changers out of the Temple. He was conscious of the evil of this practice and he knew the consequences of his acts. Yet, as one trying to do the will of God, he acted . . .

An introduction of the same passage can get off the ground with a narrative beginning:

> The feast of the passover is in progress in Jerusalem. The streets of the city are jammed with travelers and townspeople. The Temple is the scene of greatest activity for it is here that all worshipping Jews come. The priests are here attending to their duties in a perfunctory way, feeling their great importance as necessary functionnairies. The Pharisees—can you hear them almost shouting their pious prayers "to be heard of all men"? They smooth their wide phylacteries and they hold their robes above the dust in disdainful isolation. The faithful, too, are here trying to reach God through the only means they know—with sacrifices and burnt offerings. Pitiful offerings some of them, but all a poor family can afford, especially with the high prices being charged during the feast days. And worst of all there are the money-changers who have set up shops in the very Temple itself to more easily rake in their profits from the faithful who have to patronize their stalls.
>
> Into this setting walks a Galilean teacher filled with anguish and anger . . .

It will take a preacher time to select the details for an accurate and an interesting Biblical beginning but he will be rewarded with attention from the audience.

The question is often debated as to whether or not a preacher should begin a sermon by quoting a text. The concern here is not textual preaching but merely the use of a text early in the introduction. Parenthetically, it may be said that it is not essential to have a text in every sermon. It may better be omitted altogether than to have the preacher hunt for an appropriate Bible verse after the sermon is completed. But if a text is used, where and when? Generally speaking, unless the text is particularly striking it is better not to open the sermon with it. A stronger beginning is a narrative or something of special interest to the congregation, followed by the text.

Have you ever thought that it is foolish to be a Christian? When we consider the comparatively small numbers who seriously bother about religion in the world today, it does make us pause to reflect on whether or not we are wasting our time—or at least whether or not we are foolish . . . Well, this is not a new problem. St. Paul was concerned about it also. In the first chapter of I Corinthians he says, "The foolishness of God is wiser than the wisdom of men."

In this introduction, an attempt is made to arrest the attention of the audience, and then the preacher moves into the text of the sermon.

No discussion of arresting attention would be complete without mentioning the use of humor. For, although humor might be legitimately discussed in relation to the adaptation to the audience and their emotions, it does have bearing at the point of arresting attention. Humor is often used at the beginning of a sermon for the sole purpose of arousing interest. How many college students have suffered humiliation because the chapel speaker felt he must tell an unrelated funny story to get their attention before he moved into his theme! Congregations, also, are too speech-wise to be fooled by that kind of trick. Yet, humor does get attention, and if the preacher has a humorous opening which is related to his theme, and which does not jar with the mood of the service, then he may use it. Humor in the pulpit should be like a wave of wind hitting the tops of wheat in a field. Gentle and refreshing, never side-splitting or of the comedian variety. The use of humor also depends upon the personality of the preacher. Some men have the knack of using humor in a way which adds to the sermon

without destroying its dignity. Others when they try to be
humorous work too hard and the humor sticks out rather
than the point it was intended to illustrate. The most effective
use of humor in preaching is the gentle thrust in terms of
furthering the theme. Even a good humorist will use his
ability sparingly in the pulpit. It was once said of a popular
preacher, "He's the Methodists' Bob Hope." That epithet
may be too high a price to pay for the preacher who wants
to unfold the riches of God.

Whatever type of introduction the preacher chooses, it
should be relatively short. Many preachers spend too much
time getting started. It is easier to diagnose than to prescribe,
and generally easier to open up a problem than to solve it
later on in the sermon. Often unconsciously the preacher deals
in the easier of the two areas. Usually one or two paragraphs
should suffice to disclose and clarify a subject and at the same
time arrest the attention of the audience.

Why are the initial interest and attention factors so important in a sermon? For one thing, there is a tendency for
audience interest to slip at the end of the worship service.
The preacher needs to recapture it before the psychological
unit is broken. Also, an audience's attention fluctuates constantly, but there are said to be two places where a well-directed
audience listens most attentively—the beginning and the end
of a sermon. The preacher must capture those first few
moments with material that will make the congregation follow
into the sermon willingly. Finally, the first few minutes of a
sermon involve a psychological battle between the preacher
and the congregation. If the preacher is going to win, he must
control the situation with a strong beginning. If the introduction is weak, the chances are he has lost his audience before
he even gets into the sermon.

The methods of getting attention and arousing interest are
limitless; a minister will be rewarded by a study of them. As
long as he keeps his methods in good taste and in close relation
to the theme of the sermon, he may use any elements to gain
the desired end. A good beginning is part of purposeful
persuasion.

CHAPTER IV

REASON AS PERSUASION

IF A GOOD talk made a good sermon the preacher's lot would be an easier one. It is the fact that a sermon has to achieve a certain change of will that puts upon the preacher the double compulsion of knowing both the response he desires and the countless techniques which will help him achieve his goal. Persuasion becomes an art.

Because the preacher is concerned with the whole man he constantly guards against offending either man's intellect or his emotions. For many people, the more cogent, rational, and intellectual a sermon is the more persuasive it is. It is no accident that the Bible contains the text, "Come, now let us reason together." Christianity is a reasonable religion and if the Christian faith is to compete in the market place of ideas with other ideologies, then men of the pulpit must be able to articulate meaningfully the faith that is within them. The lawyer who sits in the pew and listens to his preacher present the Gospel as if he were presenting a brief before a jury may be moved to action immediately. And so may others who are not lawyers by profession. Although it is unfair to compartmentalize people into rational and emotional, it is important that the basis of every good sermon be a sound idea, then that the idea be clearly and rationally developed and presented in such a way as to appeal to the minds as well as the hearts of men.

This premise suggests that the preacher should have at least a nodding acquaintance with the canons of logic. Many laymen, after listening to preachers for years, conclude that logic might well be the minister's major area of study. Repeatedly laymen complain that their preacher is guilty of unsupported assertions, vague generalities, faulty reasoning, and lack of evidence. Granted that a sermon which is only logical might be dry as dust, no preacher in this age can afford to be unclear, incorrect, or intellectually shoddy in the pulpit.

An effective preacher understands the differences between reasoning and rationalizing; he knows the differences between fact and opinion; he respects the uses of evidence, and of forms of support. Certainly there should be concern with the place of reason in persuasion at the point where reason impinges upon the sermon: the sharpness of the idea, the structure, and the outline. These factors are the minimal concerns of logic.

How does a preacher begin to construct a sermon? The young preacher often asks the experienced minister, "Where do you get ideas for your sermons?" There is no one answer. Some preachers follow the church year, others a table of Scripture lessons. With experience the preacher begins to see sermon themes in life situations. Or during Bible study a text may leap up like a magnet attracting iron filings. The title of a book—better still the content—may stir up an idea that cannot be resisted. Elton Trueblood's *Alternative to Futility* may send a man out on the trail of a sermon. An evening with a favorite author may give the preacher the same reaction which someone expressed in regard to Walter Lippmann: "His writing is fly paper to me—if I touch it I am stuck to the finish."

A sermon idea may come from regular periods of meditation. On the other hand, some ministers find that by letting their minds lie fallow during the summer months they are filled to overflowing with themes when they take up their work again in the fall. An occasional preacher depends on getting into the proper mood. He may not go to the extreme some creative minds have found necessary but he may require something outside himself, an environmental stimulus, to help induce thought.

Rousseau would think bareheaded in full sunshine; Bossuet would work in a cold room with his head wrapped in furs; Schiller and Grétry would put their feet into ice-cold water. Beethoven in part ruined his hearing by pouring cold water over his head. Many—including Descartes, Milton, Leibnitz, Rossini, and Prescott—lay smothered under blankets, "thinking horizontally." Winston Churchill dictated his memoirs from bed each day until noon. Hume wrote his *History of England* on a sofa. Sheridan watched long and anxiously at night for bright thoughts . . . Dickens, a believer in magnetic influences, always turned his bed to the north.

Whatever may be the route by which the preacher arrives at a particular theme for Sunday morning a primary consideration is that it be clear in his own mind. There is a correlation between clarity of thinking and clarity of expression. Among the faults of modern sermons, lack of clarity probably heads the list. Many preachers seem to feel that their people have come to church to play "Point, point, who's got the point?" Occasionally, one even finds a preacher who rationalizes fuzziness. Said one: "In the sermon I try to create a mood more than anything else." Often such a statement is an excuse for slipshod thinking and an unwillingness to grasp an idea firmly, and as Jacob of old with the angel, wrestle with it.

However, there is an element of good sermon building in the desire to create a mood. The sermon does more than verbalize ideas. But if preaching is basically communication, then clear presentation of a clear idea should be primary. One aspect of preaching is similar to the conductor's calling out the stations on the train. The task may be prosaic, but if one is headed anywhere and hopes to arrive at the proper destination, then the conductor is necessary.

Categorically, the first concern of the preacher in building a sermon is to refine the subject or theme. In a sense, it is the same problem as that of the miner who seeks to extract the iron from a carload of sludge, muck, dirt, and rock. The theme has to be chiseled down to manageable size for one sermon and then given shape. Many sermons have a pointless thrust because the theme has not been sharpened—not even in the preacher's mind. Perhaps the best way to achieve clarity is to begin work on the sermon long enough in advance so that the mind can have time to grapple with the idea. The process of creative thinking needs time for the growth of an idea.

To any proposed theme it may be helpful to apply specific questions: Is this idea important? What is the truth here that needs emphasizing? Do my people need this message? How can I make it relevant? Some such questioning between the preacher and his idea should precede every sermon.

In answering these preliminary questions the preacher comes to a clear focus on the sermon; he knows why he is preaching it, and what he wants his congregation to do as a result.

Having decided upon an idea or theme a preacher will save both time and effort if he will reduce to writing the next three considerations in sermon building: the thesis, the purpose, and the response sought.

The thesis or proposition of the sermon seeks to answer the question, "What is the basic affirmation of this sermon?" For example, one preacher says to another at the Monday ministers' meeting, "What did you preach about yesterday?" If the first preacher replies "Salvation," he is giving the subject. The thesis is what he had to say about salvation. Therefore, in answer to the question, he might reply, "Salvation is the process of being changed *from* something *to* something through God's grace." In other words, the thesis is the positive affirmation of the sermon in one sentence. And it should be statable in one sentence. If a paragraph is necessary to state the thesis, the chances are that the subject is too large. It is true that the thesis will not always be evolved immediately upon thinking about the idea; occasionally the thesis will change as the sermon grows; still a definite statement of the thesis helps the preacher to keep the material sharply focused, to cut away irrelevant material, to establish the goal toward which the sermon should move.

Within the structure of the sermon the thesis is most frequently found at the climax of the sermon, near the conclusion. For example, a sermon on fear might have as its outline: I. The prevalence of fear. II. The causes of fear. III. The Christian Gospel offers help for fears. The climax of point III

—the support of the point—is no doubt the thesis of this sermon. It could be stated: "A vibrant faith in God alleviates our fears." Occasionally, though, the thesis may be stated in the introduction. The sermon "3-Dimensional Christianity" referred to earlier is an example of statement of the thesis in the introduction.

However, the placement of the thesis has little to do with its essential merit. Sometimes the thesis is never explicitly stated, only implied; but the preacher does well to have it written out for his own guidance. It would be difficult to estimate the number of sermons which would be improved if the preacher had bothered to decide clearly and early what he was talking about. Too many preachers merely construct a sermon on a general theme and let it grow. But like a flower plot, if left to grow untended, the weeds may be the winner.

Beyond the thesis, it is necessary to have the purpose of the sermon clearly in mind. Here the question is simply, "Why am I preaching this sermon?" The answer forces the preacher to examine his own motivation, to see the sermon in light of the needs of the people in front of him, and above all to keep the sermon moving in the right direction. Unfortunately, many preachers might find that their only truthful answer to the question is, "To fill up twenty minutes." There are a variety of reasons for preaching: to inform, to instruct, to inspire, to guide, to motivate, to counsel, to persuade. The purpose will determine the choice of the material, the slant of the argument, the emphasis, and the desired outcome.

If a preacher chooses to preach on a Biblical doctrine, his purpose may be simply "To explain in concrete terms the meaning of salvation." If he has that sentence before him during his preparation, it is obvious that his sermon will be aided in its direction and clarity. At another time the purpose of the sermon may arise from some specific need of the audience. For example, if through his pastoral counseling the preacher discovers that members of his congregation are anxious about many things (and this is certainly a true life situation), then his purpose may be stated, "I want my people to have an understanding of the Gospel which will help them overcome their fears." The fact that the preacher expresses the purpose—no matter how obvious or simple it may seem—gives the sermon better focus and the preacher is compelled to fulfill his purpose before he can consider the sermon finished. Although it is apparent that the purpose is closely related to the thesis, the distinction should be kept in mind. *The thesis is a statement of the major affirmation of the sermon. The purpose is the reason for making that affirmation.*

The third question which the preacher needs to answer before the sermon progresses in construction is, "What do I want these people to do? What is the response sought?" A sermon should not be preached unless the preacher has something specific in mind for the audience to do. For one thing, a specific response helps the preacher in his fervor of delivery. If he is discussing repentance, he may have as his desired response, "When these people get home I want them to think about their need for repentance." Or, the response may be, "I want as many as possible to come kneel at the altar now and repent." Those two responses would certainly affect the delivery of the sermon. The persuasive sermon, especially, demands some response, whether to change an attitude, to induce people to study, or to invite them to some action. Whatever the desired response, the act of thinking it through makes the preacher more effective.

In some cases thesis, purpose, and response are almost indistinguishable. A preacher builds a sermon on how to pray effectively. The thesis might be: Prayer involves several steps; the purpose might be to teach the listeners how to pray; and the response sought: more praying in the lives of his people. In this case these factors may seem obvious, but even here their statement gives the speaker a focus and a goal.

The following example is taken from a student paper. Even without the sermon outline which followed, the direction of the sermon can be seen.

A CONTROL OF LOVE

Text:	"For the love of Christ controls us." II Cor. 5:14
Thesis:	"The love of Christ is operative in our lives."
Purpose:	To demonstrate the effect of the love of Christ in a responsive life.
Response:	To seek a renewed devotion to the great things of life through devotion to Christ's controlling love.

With the thesis, the purpose, and the response established, the next step in sermon building is construction of the outline. Some preachers evidently do not take the matter of outlining seriously. Outlining demands laborious grappling with the idea and, therefore, is not particularly exciting to the lazy worker. Other preachers boast that they simply sit down and write out their sermons which fall "naturally" into an outline. Others claim to have a "psychological" outline. Every sermon should have a written outline to support it, to show its direction, and to make the idea crystal clear. This procedure does not mean that a preacher should be tied to a written form. It may be that after his outline is finished, one preacher will write a complete manuscript, another one will preach extemporaneously from the outline, another may never need refer to it again. How the outline is used does not matter. It has served its purpose if it has provided a logical structure for the sermon. The speaker who cannot outline or refuses to outline generally cannot think clearly. Outlining is one of the most difficult aspects of preaching, but the preacher who would be clear—and therefore persuasive—should be able to structure his ideas.

Some of the wisest words about outlining come from those old chestnuts of freshman English courses: Unity, Coherence, and Emphasis. If the outline manages to embody these three factors, then it has gone a long way in fulfilling its purpose for the sermon.

Unity: A sermon should have one basic idea—the thesis. The several points in the sermon are a breakdown of this central idea. It is not unusual to hear a preacher announce a sermon topic then proceed to discuss very unrelated ideas. He may announce his theme as "Eternal Life," but build a sermon so vague that any Christian concept could be substituted for eternal life without affecting the structure of the sermon. A brief outline will illustrate:

ETERNAL LIFE

Introduction
  I. What it is not
          A. Church membership
          B. Good Works
          C. Keeping the Golden Rule

    II. What it is
                    A. Gift
                    B. Relationship
                    C. Possession
                    D. Hope
        Conclusion

The topic for this outline could equally well have been
"The Good Life," or "Discipleship."

Occasionally a preacher will try to cover too much material
and construct an omnibus sermon. A critical study of the outline will indicate the lack of unity in such a sermon. What
could be a simple and helpful sermon on "Marks of Discipleship" can easily mushroom into something unmanageable if
it is divided into aspects which are too broad and inclusive:
I. Faith, II. Hope, III. Love. A stated thesis and purpose will
help this preacher keep the outline within limits. He should
remember also that the whole Gospel does not have to be
preached in one sermon. He will be back in the pulpit again
next Sunday.

Coherence: Coherence is concerned with the logical connection between one point and another. Some sermons do not
lead logically from one point to another, and listening to them
is like being led to the edge of a precipice without seeing a
bridge. Coherence is most obviously needed when the sermon
is built so that each point depends upon the previous one.
For example, in a sermon on Salvation, the points may build
climactically. I. Need for Salvation. II. Recognition of the
Need. III. Fulfillment of the Need. Those are the steps, and
they must logically follow one another. Even in a sermon where
the points are co-ordinate parts of a whole, coherence is necessary. "Three Cornerstones of a Happy Life" may be Peace,
Kindness, and Humility. The preacher is justified in starting
with any one of the three aspects, but he has to decide with
which one he will begin, and how he will proceed from one
section to another.

Emphasis: Emphasis has to do with spending the correct
amount of time in the right places. Many preachers are like
the proverbial trackman who spends too much time running in
one spot. A short introduction is the best start. Briefness is
also a good characteristic for the first half of most sermons.

Frequently so much time is spent setting up the problems and analyzing the ills under discussion that the preacher walks out at twelve o'clock without having said much of a constructive nature. Someone has suggested that most sermons would gain in effectiveness if two-thirds of the time were spent on the last third of the sermon. Usually a tight outline will enable the preacher to sense how much time he needs to spend in the various sections of the sermon.

The habit of using standard symbols in making an outline is helpful. Most preachers have had an adequate training in the use of these symbols and in the different outline procedures in either sentence or topic forms. Although the mechanics of outlining are important it is fair to say that they are secondary to the thinking involved in the process. However, the symbols help fix the material in the mind even as one writes them down; and when the preacher comes to deliver the sermon he can often see the structure in his mind's eye as clearly as when he worked it out in his study. It is obvious that the world's future does not hang on the use of consistent symbols—but many good sermons do! In the main, the problem of outlining reduces itself to the problem of rigorous thinking necessary to shape the content of the sermon into logical form. The following outline is an example of a working skeleton outline:

ON BEING MATURE

Introduction: (Dramatization of the following statements)

    Ours is an age seeking maturity.

    In different words St. Paul speaks of a mature mind in giving the steps of a sound Christian experience.

    Scriptural material: Phil. 3:12-15

        "Not that I have already obtained this or am already perfect . . . forgetting what lies behind . . . I press on toward the goal for the prize of the upward call of God in Christ Jesus."

    What are the marks of a mature mind?

I. RECOGNIZING OUR LIMITATIONS ("Not that I have already obtained this or am already perfect.")

    A. Paul

        1. Recognized his need ("I am chief of sinners")

        2. Recognized his shortcomings ("The good that I would that I do not")

    B. Us
        1. To have a vital Christian faith we must recognize our
           need
           a. there must be a diagnosis before one can be healthy
           b. recognition of need comes before repentance
        2. To have a vital Christian faith we must evaluate our
           limitations
           a. tragedy to expect more than what we can do ade-
             quately
           b. tragedy not to understand occasional errors
    Summary and Transition:

II. FORGETTING OUR FAILURES (". . . forgetting what lies
    behind . . .")
    A. Paul
        1. Persecution of the Christians
        2. A religion of legalism
    B. Us
        1. Not dwelling on past mistakes
        2. Essence of forgiveness
           a. religion
           b. human relationships
    Summary and transition:

III. HAVING A WORTH-WHILE GOAL ("I press on toward the
    goal for the prize of the upward call of God in Christ Jesus")
    A. Paul
        1. Earthly goals
           a. visit to Spain
           b. conversion of Gentiles
        2. Cosmic goals
           a. fellowship with Christ
           b. establishment of His Kingdom
    B. Us
        1. Goals give direction to contemporary life
           a. vocation
           b. family
        2. Goals give direction to religious life
           a. Christianity dynamic itself
           b. Christian's life should show maturing change
    Summary and transition:

Conclusion: (Paul was a prisoner at the time, but he reflected the
    mind of a mature person)
    "Not that I have already obtained this or am already perfect
    . . . forgetting what lies behind . . . I press on toward the goal
    for the prize of the upward call of God in Christ Jesus."

In this outline the introduction and the conclusion are not numbered. This does not mean they are not an integral part of the sermon. However, they serve a function somewhat different from the other sections of the outline and are not a part of the logical structure of the argument. In other words, the sermon outline is a blueprint of the development of the thesis and the development begins with point I.

Each unit in the outline should contain but one item or statement. This seems simple enough, but unfortunately it is not uncommon to hear a preacher state as one point: "We are caught in a sense of futility and need the Spirit of Christ to enable us to become our real selves." There are two ideas in that one point. To preserve the logic of the discussion each idea should be stated as a separate unit.

The material gathered under the various points should be logically subordinated; that is, everything included under one point in the outline should deal with that main point; should prove, support, or amplify it. Suppose a preacher is discussing the theme that God speaks to men. Perhaps one point is "God speaking to men in the Old Testament." Everything under that point should deal with Old Testament material.

Some preachers acquire the habit of developing a point negatively rather than positively. Occasionally this procedure may be helpful, but in general the preacher should use positive examples. Suppose he is making the point that Christian love can revitalize a man's life. Why deal largely with those people who do not have Christian love? Although a negative point may be used for contrast, it should be clinched with enough positive support to make the idea complete and persuasive.

The summaries and transitions between points are extremely important in outlining for two reasons. If transitions are not clear, the logical relationship between the points is not shown. Second, the coherence, or freeflow of the sermon, depends on smooth transitions. To use again the sermon "3-Dimensional Christianity," the three main points are: I. The past—ours is a traditional faith; II. The Present—ours is an active faith; III. The Future—ours is a hopeful faith. The summary and transition between the first and second points illustrate the importance of coherence. "While we have seen that our faith is a faith of the past, a traditional faith, it is also important to see that our faith is a faith of the present, a vital faith." Although in this case the summaries and transitions are rather obvious, it is important that the preacher employ them. They are his directional signals. An audience has a right to this help.

If the outline is carefully evolved and the illustrations tested against the point to be made, the preacher has gone a long way in presenting his material clearly. Finally, it is worth repeating that the most persuasive preacher is the clear preacher —the preacher who has grappled with an idea and has then become articulate about it.

With the basic thinking done while working out the thesis, purpose, response sought and with the outline showing the logic of the argument, the preacher is ready to fill in the supporting arguments and illustrations; to work out carefully worded transitions and summaries. The selection of good supporting material emphasizes the necessity of starting work on a sermon early enough so that there is time for the idea to grow. A preacher often selects and rejects illustrations, consults his files for poetry, cogitates at length on life situations which are pertinent to the point to be made. It is through this process of selection that the sermon material becomes refined.

There remains then the preparation of a clinching conclusion and the selection of a title. It is possible that a striking title has come to the preacher while he is working on the idea of his sermon. The title should be an attention-getter for a truly worth-while theme. At times there is a temptation to think up a striking title, jack it up and run a mediocre sermon under it. Only failure is in store for a sermon that promises much and delivers little.

Finally, the preacher is ready to write his sermon in manuscript form if that is his practice, or to think it through carefully for extemporaneous presentation. Whatever is his method he will profit from verbalizing the sermon out loud—from the outline rather than the manuscript. A good sermon is the result of a long and thoughtful process. Ideas can be thrown together in a careless fashion, certainly, but the preacher who seeks to be persuasive in presenting the Word of God has not undertaken a quick or an easy task.

CHAPTER V

EMOTION AS PERSUASION

EMOTION, when applied to preaching, is a word with dangerous connotations. Unfortunately, many people equate persuasion with emotion. They feel that persuaders appeal to the so-called baser elements in man, that they operate in terms of the high-pressure salesman, the volatile revivalist, or the pyrotechnic politician.

There are two extreme attitudes toward the use of emotion in preaching. At one extreme is the minister who preaches the Gospel only on the emotional level. He not only proclaims with fervor, but he selects his material from stereotypes, pious phraseology, and the nonrational, aiming at the congregation's feelings, seeking to arouse only an emotional response. He tends either to look down upon the logical and the rational or at least to ignore them. In fact, some preachers boast that religion is not intellectual, and they consider reasonable approaches to Christianity almost unorthodox.

At the other extreme, possibly in revolt against the former, is the minister who has little to do with emotion in preaching. He may feel that emotional preaching is crude and crass, used by charlatans to get preconceived responses from people by stirring up their feelings. He considers this type of procedure unethical, preferring to present his material in an intelligent and logical manner, to appeal to the minds of men, forgetting that persuasion needs to be not only convincing but moving.

Nevertheless, it is a misconception to speak of persuasion as dealing only with the nonrational or the emotional. Persuasion takes man as he is—a dynamic being with emotions *and* intellect—and deals with him on this basis. In that sense, persuasion is concerned with the whole man.

The story of the Reverend Mr. Jones is a composite of hundreds of modern-day preachers. Mr. Jones grew up in an area where religion was thought of almost entirely in terms of the emotions. He listened to preachers haranguing their congregations, driving at their sense of sinfulness, stirring up their passions and, in short, reducing religion to something of a psychological wrenching of their entire beings. Some good came from this emotional approach. Many people responded, led better lives, and felt that God had in truth entered their lives in a significant way. But Mr. Jones, even though recognizing the good, revolted against religion thus divorced from reasonable appeals. He could not explain what happened when his own psychical make-up was trampled by the high-pressure methods of an itinerant evangelist. So Mr. Jones went to college and seminary with a distaste for emotionalism in religion. His desire was to be logical and rational; to preach so that his sermons would appeal to men's minds and not their hearts. Later, in his own pulpit he even went so far as to refrain from quoting poetry, for poetry was sentimental. He preached dispassionately, so that his listeners would respond through their higher natures, their intellects.

The Reverend Mr. Jones reflects the misconceptions of preaching found in many pulpits today. His fear of emotion blinded him to its reality. He failed to realize that there is a difference between emotion and emotionalism, between sentiment and sentimentality. He demonstrated a prevalent ignorance of the place of emotion in man's life, a kind of ignorance that allows some preachers to let emotionalism go unbridled in their pulpits and places unnecessary restraints on others. Frequently these latter men are not only afraid of emotionalism, but afraid of themselves as well; afraid that any show of emotion will tag them as ignorant, uncultivated, and neurotic.

We have rather generally turned the emotions over to the entertainment field. People go to the movies and expect to laugh and cry. They listen to a symphony, and expect to be moved. They go to a play, and expect their emotions to be aroused, else they criticize the play as being inadequate. Yet in the church they expect the emotions to be untouched. Congregations do not desire the preacher to "stir them up." Then the preacher, afraid to be his real self in the pulpit, is frustrated because he does not reach the wellsprings of behavior within his people. If, after an effective sermon, someone were to come up and kneel at the altar the modern preacher would be caught off guard. The tragedy is that the preacher who keeps all emotion out of his preaching is not communicating on a deep and important level in the interaction between human beings.

To suggest that emotions should be a vital part of preaching does not mean that the preacher should use tear-jerking stories, a special ministerial tone, and pious phraseology. It does mean that he should be concerned that his material is presented in a warmly human manner; that he reveal the concerns of love and the other emotions which support his message. His manner, delivery, and material should reflect the deep feelings which not only support what he is saying, but which in truth say something themselves in a way that mere verbalization cannot. This combination produces persuasive preaching; it is communication at its highest.

The preacher who realizes that members of the congregation listen to a sermon with their whole being will not only verbalize words, but will communicate also emotions and feelings. To move an audience to the response sought in a particular sermon, a preacher may state that "God gives us freedom, but our highest freedom comes when we choose His will for our lives." This idea would have conviction and persuasive power only if he followed the statement with a moving example with which the congregation could identify themselves. A family illustration showing how the child can be given freedom, but becomes his most mature self in returning that freedom to the family in terms of responsibility, would make the proposition concrete.

A preacher communicates on a nonverbal as well as a verbal level. If he speaks of love and at the same time frowns, if his voice is harsh and his manner cold, then he is not supporting his verbalizations. Conversely, when he speaks of love, his manner, voice, and basic attitude should reflect that emotion. In this regard, a sermon is like an iceberg; much of its impact lies below the surface.

The emotional well-being of the preacher himself is of great importance. His inadequacies, fears, and insecurities are almost impossible to keep out of his preaching, for they are revealed in delivery, pulpit presence, and general attitude. They may be revealed also in less discernible and more covert ways. A set jaw, fleeting eyes, a tentative, hesitant, or creaking voice may reveal that the preacher's own emotional life has insecurities. To be sure, one should not assume that there is a set way for preachers to smile, act, and sound, for the uniqueness of an individual is an important asset. Many preachers with bad habits in the pulpit compensate for them in some other way and are effective in their preaching. Perhaps it is possible for a preacher with emotional difficulties to be effective; but by and large, a healthy emotional life is necessary if he is to be persuasive, for he is revealing himself and is communicating on that level as well as upon the verbal level.

Furthermore, the use of emotion is important in persuasive preaching because the emotions are at the center of volition. In order to effect a response, the emotions need to be reached. They are the center of action. It is possible to convince a person on the verbal level of the truth of a certain proposition or idea, but to get him to act upon that idea in a meaningful way, he must be touched where he is motivated in the emotions. For instance, from a rational standpoint a person may see the need for giving to the March of Dimes, yet not be moved to do so. But if he can be made to feel what life would be like if his own son had polio, then he can be moved to contribute. In persuasive preaching where a specific response is being sought the utilization of the emotions is imperative.

Today a large body of knowledge relating to the emotions is available. Its mastery makes great demands on the preacher, but if preaching the Word of God is important, these demands are not too much to expect from the faithful minister of Jesus

Christ. To understand the emotions enables the preacher to understand the people of his congregation, to grasp their mental attitudes and mind sets. Strictly speaking, these attitudes are not emotional but they reflect the emotional manner in which an audience may respond to a speaker's ideas.

First of all, a preacher needs to understand the factor of rationalization and its tremendous importance in the preaching situation. Rationalization is the process whereby a person justifies or promotes a belief, wish, or action which he believes is essential to his own well-being. It is the pathway many people tread in arriving at their mental attitudes. As contrasted with reason, rationalization begins with a wish or a desire and then seeks to find support for the attitude. A man desires a new car! He begins with his wish and then lines up arguments to support it. The old car has depreciated greatly; soon it will need major repairs; the safety devices on the new cars will protect his loved ones. And so down the line. In the field of religion this same kind of wishful thinking is evidenced when a man who habitually loses his temper rationalizes the habit as being the result of repeated righteous indignation. The preacher must be aware of this tendency to rationalize in order to understand some of his own motives, as well as the mental attitudes of the congregation. Usually rationalization is used to offset failure, to shirk responsibility, to justify some prejudice, or to build support for some decision already made.

Rationalization is not in the same category as the processes commonly called emotional, but it is definitely "nonrational" and ultimately derives from some wish which, technically speaking, could be called emotional. An understanding of this process of "thinking" enables the preacher to adapt his material to the thought patterns of the congregation. For example, if he is dealing with the problem of race prejudice in an area where there is a well-grounded prejudice against another group, it is important for him to realize that such prejudice often begins with a fear and threat to one's well-being. Then follows a process of rationalization designed to justify that fear or threat. The preacher has a better chance to deal with the prejudice if he knows how it has been developed.

Another type of pseudo-thinking closely allied to rationalization is the stereotype process. Stereotypes are pictures in the mind which seek to comprise the entire order of things. These pictures arise from previous experiences, or desires, or pressure groups, or habitual ways of looking at things. New ideas are accepted or rejected on the basis of their relationship to this preconditioned picture. "Jews are tight-fisted," "Negroes are shiftless," "New Englanders are cold and aloof," are a few of the familiar slogans which exemplify stereotyped thinking. Although stereotypes have important implications for language and persuasion, they are also important in relation to the emotions, for many times one's emotional conditioning affects his receptivity of an idea and is the basis of his stereotypes.

The preacher faces stereotype thinking in many forms. A harmless illustration in a sermon may "trigger" a stereotyped response from his congregation. Some word he uses fits into the congregation's stereotype of "fundamentalist," "liberal," "right-winger." A preacher who speaks out on racial prejudice may find that this issue fits into the stereotype of left-wing influences, and he is called "pink."

In combating stereotype thinking the preacher needs to adapt his material to his congregation. Not that he adjusts his message and material to fit the stereotypes, but rather that he is careful in his use of language and illustrations to avoid words and materials which lend themselves to thoughtless stereotyping.

A third factor in this area of persuasive preaching is the use of suggestion. Suggestion is the process of gaining response by establishing an idea in the mind of another person—usually in the marginal field of his attention. Every speaker, consciously or unconsciously, uses suggestion both in speech content and in delivery. With a little thought the preacher can make effective use of this element.

Suggestion is at work through the preacher's appearance, posture, attitude toward the audience, method of delivery, the language in which the sermon is couched. It is to be hoped that all these elements are positive in their impact upon the congregation, establishing the idea the preacher desires to develop. The speaker who is well-informed, who communicates his ideas with confidence in himself and his message, is sure to set off positive responses in the minds of the congregation.

There is suggestion at work in the very nature of the ideas a preacher dwells upon. If he speaks of the love of God, the help and sustenance of religion, he is suggesting positively the merits of the Christian life. The message itself may carry a judgment upon the people, but their mind is set to receive the message because they have been conditioned to a positive response.

Language is important in creating positive responses. A filling-station attendant who comes to the car, begins to wipe the windshield, and inquires, "Fill 'er up?" is creating a positive response in the driver's mind, so that it is easy for him to say, "Sure." Otherwise, he must break down the positive "sure" already suggested and think up reasons to say, "No, only two gallons." In the same way a congregation is impressed and reacts in a certain way because of factors which are not always consciously analyzed by them.

An overdose of positive suggestion may cause a negative reaction and establish a response the speaker does not desire because it eventuates in a recoil from the idea presented. A high-pressure salesman who contends constantly that a suit was made for the customer, fits to a T, is exactly the right color, often loses the sale because of overflattery. Likewise a preacher may create a negative response by his actions, language, ideas, and delivery. At times, neither the audience nor the preacher is aware of the cause of the negative reaction. The conscientious preacher is concerned with all elements that condition responses and endeavors to make the total impact of his sermon positive.

Repeated scrutiny of the nature of his ideas helps a preacher to see if his primary emphasis is upon the negative or the positive aspects of the Gospel. If he continually stresses the sins of the congregation or casts the Gospel message in terms of "don'ts," then the impact in the long run will be negative. Of course, the preacher will speak on such themes, but he can deal with negative aspects of the Gospel in a positive way. The people should be convicted of their sins, but the saving truth of the Gospel is redemption. A sermon which spends its entire time in convicting the congregation of sin, falls short because it leaves out the note of salvation.

The language of the preacher may be negative, sometimes inadvertently so. It might be well for him to go over his sermons and note the amount of negative language he has used. Replaying a tape recording of an occasional sermon helps the preacher discover if there is an inordinate amount of "don't do this" or "don't do that." Making religion consist of a series of taboos has the same effect as constant use of negatives.

In addition to causing a negative response through the language of a sermon, the preacher may get a negative reaction from his delivery. If he has a weak voice, is timid and afraid, hesitant and insecure, he sets up the wrong response; the audience becomes embarrassed for him and concentrates more on his weakness than on the message itself.

An opening apology is a negative approach. "I hope you will bear with me, for I have a terrible cold"; or "Our little boy was ill last night, so I am afraid I am not well prepared this morning." Whereas the preacher hopes to elicit sympathy, in reality he is causing the congregation to think, "Why did he leave his sermon till Saturday night?" A congregation always regrets personal discomfort on the part of the preacher; it is always most sympathetic in the case of illness in the family, but the concern and the sympathy should not be solicited from the pulpit. If the preacher is able to be in the pulpit at all he should preach to the best of his ability without extraneous remarks, especially if those remarks are negative in their impact and cause the congregation to lose interest in the message to be proclaimed.

Following close upon the use of suggestion in a sermon is the factor of motivation. Motivation is simply the method by which the congregation is led to act as the preacher desires, and the primary purpose of preaching is to gain a favorable response to a given thesis. Although the basic appeal is to the emotions, motivation is not divorced from the intellectual or the rational. All speakers try to get the audience to respond to the proposition set forth. It may be a general response sought, such as "Look favorably upon religion," or it may be a specific response, such as "Turn your life around and make a decision for Christ." Whatever the response, the persuasive preacher is concerned with the whole process of motivation, how it works in a congregation, and how he himself can use it in his preaching.

If the preacher understands the place of emotion in the lives of normal people he will be able to balance intellectual and emotional appeals in his preaching. He will not become an either-or but a both-and; he will develop the ability to minister to people as individuals with needs that vary and with problems that they must cope with on different levels, at times intellectual and at times emotional.

CHAPTER VI

DRAMATIZING THE IDEA

THE MAJOR task of the preacher is to make the essentials of the Christian faith—God, Christ, the Holy Spirit, prayer—"come alive" to his people. He is dealing, therefore, with the intangible, the spiritual, the unseen, the abstract.

It is often difficult to make these concepts *live* in the lives of ordinary human beings. Many times the preacher does not succeed, partly because of the basic difficulty in articulating spiritual matters and partly because the habit of high-altitude flying is deeply engrained in the pulpit. The preacher faces people who are confronted by fears, anxieties, and joys, but they are also confronted by such tangibles as alarm clocks, automobiles, razor blades, pots and pans. These concrete things are often nearer their understanding and interest than are the concepts with which the preacher is prone to deal.

Walter Lippmann has provided a good text for preachers to take unto themselves: "People think with pictures in their heads." Once he accepts the truth of this statement, a speaker begins to realize the importance of dramatizing an idea so that he and the congregation see the same picture. The basic principle of dramatization is to place truth in such imaginative form that people respond through several of their senses. For the preacher, it means presenting the Gospel in such a way that people respond to it with their whole being—they virtually participate in the Gospel itself. When a preacher presents the Gospel in dramatic form he and the congregation participate together; the sermon becomes a shared experience in which all are vital participants in the drama unfolding before their eyes.

Soren Kierkegaard points out that the speaker is not an actor, and the listeners are not theatergoers who pass judgment upon the actor. Rather, the speaker is the prompter who whispers lines to the audience; they are the actors before God, who is the critic-judge. To the extent that the audience is a vital factor in the sermon, this analogy has bearing on the process of dramatizing the idea. In this sense the word "drama" is not synonymous with the theater. It is not suggested that the preacher become a center of spotlight attention. Contrived devices such as shifting lights, colored lights, striking poses, and long pauses—these theatricals dramatize the preacher, not the idea.

Nor is the preacher merely a storyteller. Although narrative is a vital part of dramatizing an idea, the stringing together of stories does not constitute a sermon. There are still preachers who, having selected a theme, comb their files, magazines, books of anecdotes and other helps for stories which pertain to the topic and then loosely string together these stories without consideration for arriving at a given destination. True, these verbal offerings often have an effect upon an audience because the stories themselves are dramatic enough to arouse the emotions. Hence, the preacher may be deceived into believing he has done a great work because he has his listeners laughing and crying all through the sermon. Any effective public speaker can get on his feet with a bundle of stories and emotion-laden incidents and reach the people. But is that preaching? If so, Jimmy Durante should be ordained immediately. A good story is valuable to a preacher only if it helps him to communicate an idea for some meaningful purpose.

The caution against the use of theatricals in the pulpit is no indictment of the theater. It is making its positive contribution to our social order; some of the best presentations of the Christian message are being given in the theater today. Hundreds untouched by the church have been reached by T. S. Eliot, Cristopher Fry, and others. One may not always agree with some of the underlying theology but it is important to note that these writers present the Gospel message in the real-life situations of our times, and that people respond as they do not respond to the outmoded settings and abstract affirmations which characterize much of today's preaching.

Many local churches still have a fear of professional drama in the church. One theologian commented that he believed T. S. Eliot had most of the Gospel in his play, *The Cocktail Party*, yet a local church objected to a review of the book because of its title. In this modern comedy of manners Eliot attempts to solve the dilemma of finding spiritual meaning in a materialistic world. One resolution is suggested by Eliot's worldly couple who "learn to make the best of a bad job, and carry on at a cocktail party, adjusted in humility to a world without spirit or meaning."[1] Another resolution is presented by a young woman who suffers from a sense of sin and seeks to reject both herself and the world by going into foreign mission service and being martyred. New wineskins for the old wine of the Gospel? If they seem too strange, what an indictment on those entrusted with the Word!

The Christian Church is not a johnny-come-lately to the theater. In the tenth century dramatic action was introduced into the Church to give meaning to the Mass, especially at Christmas and Easter. Since these early portrayals dealt with the great mysteries they were called mystery plays. Later the miracle plays depicted the spiritual powers attributed to the saints. Then morality plays sought to show the struggle between good and evil. Still later, as the play became secularized, the Church and the play parted company and the drama which had come into being to give illiterate people spiritual insight into Gospel truths moved from the altar to the church steps and finally to the village green. However, the modern church need not look askance at the playwright. It might better kneel in repentance that it allowed the most moving manner of presenting an idea to slip from its grasp.

[1] S. H. Hopper (ed.), *Spiritual Problems in Contemporary Literature*: George R. Kernodle, "Patterns of Belief in Contemporary Drama," New York, Harper, 1952, pp. 204-5.

In speaking of the role of the spectator in the theater Arthur Miller[2] says:

> . . . he must . . . *discover*. And if there happens to be something real up there, something human, something true, our visitor may come away with a new feeling in his heart, a sense of having been part of something quite extraordinary and even beautiful . . . he may feel he has been present at an *occasion*. For outside this theater, no one in the world heard what he heard or saw this night. I know that, for myself, there is nothing so immediate, so actual as an excellent performance of an excellent play. I have never known the smell of sweat in a movie house. I have known it in the theater—and they are also airconditioned. *Nor have I known in a movie house the kind of audience unity that occasionally is created in the theater, an air of oneness among strangers that is possible in only one other gathering place—a church.* [Italics added.]

If Miller is right then the preacher can see the possibilities of preaching which seeks to enfold the congregation into a unit. He can present a great message in which they participate, see themselves, their sins, their needs, and even more, their redemption. A man who does this kind of preaching is not only dramatizing the idea; more important, he may be a channel through which God can change men's lives.

Specifically, how is one to go about presenting the Gospel in a dramatic way? The first step is to understand the nature of the Gospel itself. It is a story full of human experience: a Father who loved his children, all of them; a baby born into a family with problems, with worries for the mother, father, and brothers; a young man growing up with the temptations that beset other young men; a decision and a life dedication; a short ministry; death upon a cross; then victory over death. This is the Great Drama which is the heart of faith.

In addition to its central message the Bible offers many stories which aid the preacher in presenting the basic truths of Christianity. The story of Job dramatizes the dilemmas and problem of suffering. If the preacher and the congregation can live with Job in his agony, can identify themselves with the friends who come to argue with him, can suffer through to

2 Arthur Miller, "The American Theater," *Holiday*, Vol. 17, No. 1, Jan., 1955, p. 92.

a victorious faith in God, they have achieved a new faith. Hosea's vivid portrayal of the demands of love offers another truth concerning the relationship between God and man.

The culmination of the dramatic method is seen in Jesus' parables as conveyers of truth. Because of their universality and their human appeal many of the parables are stronger protagonists for the Gospel than any book of theology on the same theme. The lost coin, the mustard seed, the pearl of great price—all are pictorial and all are based upon common experiences. Within the parable of the prodigal son is undoubtedly the truth of the entire Gospel: sin, redemption, grace, love, and salvation.

The Gospel is never a static set of principles about religion; it is a vivid, moving, aresting experience that includes the most important matters of human existence—concerns which face each of us today. That is the reason why the persuasive preacher preaches the Gospel, not about the Gospel. The lines of Archibald MacLeish are relevant:

> A poem should not mean
> But be[3]

In the same way a sermon should not merely mean, but should also exist. The early Christians were arrested by the great and dramatic event of Christ's Resurrection, and men today are in turn arrested by the dramatic events of their lives in response to the Great Drama. Simply stated, the Bible gives a dramatic rendering of truth rather than an exposition of it.

Church history, recording the lives of such men as Hus, Luther, and Wesley, provides vivid dramatizations which buttress the truth of our Gospel. Just as the preacher draws from the Bible, so also the figures and events of church history become his province.

Dramatization of the Gospel truths begins with the preacher himself. What he is as pastor, counselor, administrator, husband, father, friend—these all come to bear on his sermon on Sunday morning. His whole life is a dramatization of what he actually believes and must coincide with what he preaches on Sunday if that preaching is to be meaningful. We read in

[3] *Ars Poetica.* Boston, Houghton Mifflin. Used by permission.

the Gospels that "Jesus went about doing good." More people today, as was true in His time, respond to the daily touch of His life on others than respond to the abstract teaching of even so fine a discourse as the Sermon on the Mount.

When and how to dramatize his central idea—this is the preacher's problem. Having decided upon the theme or idea for a sermon he is faced with the question how best to present his thought. He then accommodates his style of presentation to the type of sermon he is to preach. The unhurried exposition, the detailed exegesis, the inexorable step-upon-step of argument—all these are the opposite of dramatization which depends upon vivid scenes, changes in tempo, identification of the spectator with the characters in the story. The preacher's delivery needs always to be under control but his imagination can lead his congregation far from the scenes of ordinary living. For instance, as the preacher and the congregation become part of the stirring scene in which Isaiah is called before the Lord, they see the throne high and lifted up in its majestic splendor, they hear the seraphim crying, "Holy, holy, holy is Jehovah of hosts!" They feel the shaking foundations as the voice fills the Temple. They suffer the consternation of Isaiah as he cries out, "Woe is me!" The cleansing coals of fire touch their lips as well as Isaiah's, and when God asks, "Whom shall I send?" they respond with Isaiah in calm resolution, "Here am I; send me." Erased are the thousands of miles and the hundreds of years between Isaiah in the Temple and the American sitting in an ultramodern church. If the preacher has caught the drama of the story his people actually live for a few minutes with the ancient prophet—and God.

We speak today of the miracle of the new drugs, and recount dramatic recoveries due to their uses. There were also miracles of Jesus' healing in which the drama lay in what happened after the miracle. Jesus' healing of the ten lepers outside the gates of Jerusalem is a moving story. A congregation can be led to see the approach of the Master and his disciples, to hear the cries of "Unclean! unclean!" from the outcast lepers sitting among the rocks, to watch Jesus as he stops to look with compassion upon them. Then the miracle of healing. The swift departure of the cleansed men. And the climax when one returns to give him thanks. They hear Jesus as he asks, "Were there not ten men? Where are the other nine?"

The preacher who has a gift for storytelling or dramatization is sometimes tempted to rely upon the method rather than the idea. There is always the Reverend Mr. Scheherazade with his thousand and one Sundays of stories. He discovers a good story and includes it in a sermon because he likes the story. The congregation may respond to the illustration and even go away remembering the story, but unless it has led them to the point the preacher is making the illustration has failed. An illustration is a window that lets in light on the theme under discussion.

Since it is easier to visualize the familiar than the unfamiliar the preacher needs to relate his material to the nature of the congregation before him. But he must be sure he understands the connotations of the words used and is accurate in the scenes presented. The preacher who was a guest at dinner and excused himself from eating squab because "I don't like fish" often has his counterpart in the pulpit. A young preacher delivering a sermon to a rural congregation chose the 23rd Psalm for the basis of his talk. He spent most of his sermon time describing sheep and their habits, then shepherds and their characteristics. Thinking he had "done himself proud" he was later abashed to have a gnarled old man ask him, "Young man, did you ever tend sheep?"

It is a false premise to suppose that only those illustrations that are within the province of a group's experience are valid in sermonizing. Some stories and experiences are universal in their appeal and if properly presented carry an audience far, in both time and space, in identifying themselves with the brotherhood of man. To quote from Plato for the sake of injecting Plato into a sermon may be sterile illustrating. But the preacher who can live in Plato's *Dialogues* and suffer and exalt with Socrates may find unexcelled drama in some of the experiences. Consider Socrates' trial before the jury of Athenians, his calm adherence to truth as he sees it, his loving forgiveness of those who pass the death sentence upon him; then follow him and his disciples into the jail room and watch with the little group of friends as their master drinks his poison; note Socrates' concern for his friends and his calmness as he makes the transition into another world—an immortality which he believed and taught. There is no greater drama than Socrates' search for truth and adherence to it. Well may a congregation feel with a disciple that "of all men of his time whom I have known, he was the wisest and justest and best."

A congregation which has lived with Socrates through his final hour will bridge the gap of centuries to another Master and His disciples, to another trial and another testimony that here was a Man of unequaled perfection. The dramatic representation of any great life is an extension forward or backward in time of the Gospel message. Illustrations which reflect universality of truth and experience may be drawn from family situations, individual sacrifice, group reactions—in short from life itself. Jesus drew upon the lilies of the field, the birds of the air, the sower, the shepherd.

Obviously, the preacher understands best what is closest to him. Therefore, from his own realm of experience he will often draw illustrations. The effectiveness of the personal illustration is at least partly due to the fact that the sermon, the preacher, and the congregation are all tied together in a joint enterprise. Dr. Gene E. Bartlett, of the First Baptist Church, Los Angeles, is a master of this type of illustration. In one of his sermons he says:

Some years ago in driving to the West Coast with the family we were all relaxed and enjoying the early evening. Then someone in the car asked, "Are you sure you are on the right road?" I replied hurriedly, "Yes, of course, this is the right road." But the question remained. Was it? And as the question found its mark something happened to all of us. We became tense, leaned forward a little, peered out the window, grew silent as we watched for some sign that would identify our road. Now, I do wish I had some dramatic end to this story. I just stopped at a service station and asked! When we found that it was the right road, there was another transformation. We all relaxed. We began to see the scenery again. Conversation was resumed as we rediscovered each other. It was the same car, the same road, the same people. One thing had happened. Meaning had been lost; and meaning had been regained.

The discretion needed in the use of personal experiences cannot be overemphasized. A preacher is sometimes tempted to draw illustrations from his parish. In an effort to be personal and to set forth life situations he reveals incidents from his calling and counseling sessions. The result is that he destroys the people's confidence in him as a man to whom they can go with their deep personal problems. It is the personal experience that can be related with propriety that is an effective means of persuasion.

If there are limits to the use of personal experience so are there limits to the use of "canned" illustrations. Stories gleaned from homiletic helps usually sound contrived and lack the ring of spontaneity. In fact, many of them sound as if they never could have happened. When a preacher cultivates the habit of asking, "How can I best make this point?" he will set out on his own. He may choose a personal illustration, he may use a hypothetical one, he may glean one from his reading. In any case, it will be his own and it will be fresh. There is a proprietary thrill in using something one has discovered. Like the prospector going over the landscape with a Geiger counter looking for uranium, so can the preacher seek fresh minerals for his illustrative material. And what is more, he will get the same thrill as the prospector when ore is discovered.

A consideration of the conclusion to a sermon has a rightful place in any study of the dramatic aspects of preaching. Drama and the conclusion have one thing in common—they should motivate the hearer. In addition, the conclusion serves the very obvious purpose of ending a sermon. If it were not so tragic it would be humorous to see how many preachers overlook this aspect of a conclusion! Frequently a preacher passes up several good opportunities to quit preaching, then suddenly glances at his watch and comes to an abrupt stop. He may have the presence of mind to raise a closing question: "Will you, like the saints of old, have this faith?" Or he may ungracefully conclude: "Let us pray." A question or a prayer may be the best ending but only if they are carefully planned to round out the pattern or structure of the sermon. They are usually poor devices if they are the brakes suddenly applied to a sermon.

As far as audience interest is concerned, the conclusion, with the introduction, share the most important places in a sermon. The conclusion should bring all thrusts of thought together in one swift, brief impact. No new ideas should be added, but the attention focused on the thesis as summary of the sermon. The second purpose of the conclusion is to motivate the congregation to action, belief, or agreement. The degree of motivation may vary. Sometimes the sermon may simply raise questions which are to be thought about by the people; sometimes it may have a specific application: "Each one bring one next Sunday." Or it may stir an emotional motivation as evidenced in an altar call or a plea for Christian discipleship. Whatever the motivation, the conclusion should answer the questions, "How?" and "So what?"

One of the major problems in preaching is the penchant for analyzing, describing, and dissecting without the restorative process of helping the people solve the problems raised in the sermon. After the preacher has aroused the people emotionally, he may suggest no way for them to respond. Granting the extravagances of revivalism, the evangelist was often more effective than some of his better-educated brethren, because he gave the people an outlet for their emotions. Whatever the approach used, it is important for the conclusion to motivate the congregation if the sermon is to be persuasive.

Three main types of conclusions are commonly used. Each is effective either in ending the sermon or in motivating the congregation, but does not usually perform both functions. The summary conclusion is a formal recapitulation of the main points made, or perhaps a paraphrase of the main points, or even an epigrammatic statement. A conclusion of application allows the preacher to ask for some specific action (overt or covert) on the part of the congregation. The third type is specifically designed to motivate. Here the preacher touches the wellsprings of emotional behavior in order to gain the response he seeks. He may use a life-situation illustration of a person meeting victoriously in a Christian way some problem facing him. The congregation then is to be motivated by self-identification with the character in the incident. Perhaps the most persuasive conclusion serves as a combination of summary and motivation and often application—the dramatized idea. It is usually narrative in form and holds up a situation in which the congregation can participate imaginatively.

In a sermon entitled "Which Way to God?" dealing with the nature of Christian experience, the preacher sought to show that there are at least three distinctive types of Christian experience. One, the emotional, dramatized in the story of St. Paul's conversion. Two, the intellectual, based on the story of Philip and the eunuch. Three, the Christian nurture approach symbolized in the Christian experience of Timothy, who grew into the faith. The conclusion was as follows:

Everything I have been saying this morning can be dramatized in the life of John Wesley. Wesley was a young Oxford don, a priest, and one of the most brilliant men of his time. His entry into the ministry was largely through an intellectual faith. But that did not satisfy him. It was the Aldersgate experience which put the warmth into his faith and sent him out to turn England upside down. Yet, even this does not tell the whole story. Back of every decision in Wesley's life was the little parsonage at Epworth and especially the faith gained through the love of his mother, Susanna Wesley. It was not until all of these were blended together that Wesley could be said to have had a mature faith.

Or take the sermon on "How Can We Know God?" delivered before a college group. The preacher sought to show that to know God means more than apprehending Him on a cognitive level. Knowing God means fellowship with Him and thus a personal relationship is established. Here is the conclusion:

This relationship between God and man on the deepest level can be demonstrated in an analogy of the relationship between two friends. Suppose while in school you have been told of someone you should meet. Maybe he is a prospective candidate for the fraternity, or a friend of your family. You know *about* him; his qualities, his attributes and something of his personality.

But then you're introduced and become casual friends. Then maybe roommates. Now there is a different relationship. You share experiences; your personalities blend. A bond grows which transcends your former knowledge. You sense the other's likes and dislikes, moods and tastes. You give of yourself to this friendship and thus, become your self because you are accepted. You are forgiven, loved, and even though you feel obligations toward the friendship they are given cheerfully because you have found someone with whom you can be your real self.

In a very real sense our relationship to God is of the same quality.

Finally, here is a conclusion taken from Herbert Butterfield's book, *Christianity and History*. This quotation would serve as a conclusion for a sermon on the Providence of God, with the thesis that the ultimate victory belongs with God:

We might say that this human story is like a piece of orchestral music that we are playing over for the first time. In our presumption we may act as though we were the composer of the piece or try to bring out our own particular part as the leading one. But in reality I personally only see the part of, shall we say, the second clarinet and of course even within the limits of that I never know what is coming after the page that now lies open before me. None of us can know what the whole score amounts to except as far as we have already played it over together, and even so the meaning of a passage may not be clear all at once. . . . If I am sure that B flat is the next note that I have to play I can never feel certain that it will not come with surprising implications until I have heard what the other people are going to play at the same moment. And no single person in the orchestra can have any idea when or where this piece is going to end.

But we can have faith that the composer of the piece will help us sound the last chord in a final harmony.[4]

All of these examples seek to focus the thesis and to motivate the congregation by dramatizing the idea. If it is true that people think with pictures in their heads, then the preacher has a specific responsibility to know for himself the Great Dramatic Event and to reveal it in the most persuasive way.

[4] Herbert Butterfield, *Christianity and History*, London, G. Bell, 1949, p. 94.

CHAPTER VII

LANGUAGE OF PERSUASION[1]

An apt illustration of the importance of words and language is suggested by the radio show, "Candid Microphone." Here questions are asked of individuals on the street and a concealed microphone picks up their comments. On one occasion the announcer stood in front of Marshall Field's and told the people who were about to enter that the building was "retroactive." It was amazing to discover how many were deterred from going into the store.

This experiment not only discloses confusion in the meaning of two similar and perhaps difficult words, but it also says something about the power of words and their influence on men's behavior. We smile at the unsophisticated reaction above, but we may buy toothpaste because it contains "irium" or hair tonic because of "lanolin" without having the foggiest notion as to what these ingredients are.

The late Dr. Irving Lee of Northwestern University, an authority in the field of general semantics, tells of an experiment in which a whispering campaign was started in an audience before a speaker began his address. The people were told that the speaker was "socialistic-minded." The speaker then gave an ultraconservative talk. Lee said, "We can predict

[1] A portion of this chapter appeared as an article, "The Libel of Labels," in *The Pastor*, Vol. 17, No. 5, Jan., 1954. Copyright, 1954, by The Pastor, and used by permission.

almost with certainty the outcome. The overwhelming majority will say the speaker's remarks were left-wing." They did. "Radical tendencies" were detected by many of his hearers.

Daily we see indications that there is such a climate of opinion, that many people are caught up in just such a maze of uncritical thinking. In a time when labels are thrown around indiscriminately, the preacher needs to be aware of some of the principles of thinking which are being violated; aware, too, of the use of words as labels and their power as symbols.

First, labels block communication. When a person is pasted with a certain label there is no need for further discussion of the merits of his ideas. Everything about him is seen in relation to that label. A friendly discussion is often halted when some phrase like "that sounds socialistic to me" is dropped into the conversation. Because an individual does not want to be stigmatized the tendency is for him to close up; communication is ended. The subject under discussion becomes taboo; the two individuals never really get a chance to understand each other.

Second, if labels stop communication, it is easy to see that they also stop thinking. A label represents a conclusion; what more is there to consider? It is easier to pull a "dangerous" book out of the library than to read it. Let a man be referred to as a "Wall Streeter" and everyone can analyze his attitudes right down the line. Let slip the fact that he is said to be pink and everyone knows he is not to be trusted.

Third, labels tend to force a man into an either-or position. They tend to be halos or stigmas; no middle way. Politically, a label forces an individual to be either a conservative or a liberal; religiously, a literalist or a heretic; socially, a modern or an old fogey. Obviously there is danger in fence-straddling or playing it safe, but many issues do not lend themselves to an easy dichotomy. Who has not heard a discussion on pacifism where each participant is pushed to the place where he has to take his stand either as an absolute pacifist or as an absolute militarist?

Fourth, labels trigger emotional responses that cloud the brain. "Socialist," "reactionary," "Progressive," or any such loose words call up definite emotional responses. Just as Pavlov's dog responded with saliva when the dinner bell rang, so people often unconsciously react emotionally and physically when labels are flung about. This principle operates both for the labeler and the labeled. Many times a discussion of politics stops when someone says, "You're a one-worlder," and another shouts, "You're an isolationist." Two men, perfectly rational one minute, are emotional fanatics the next.

What are the implications in these principles for Christian ministers? Preachers with their religious jargon can slip into thoughtless errors. On the most elementary level, most preachers have a tendency to use words that make them almost uncommunicative to their people—and often to one another. The common word "inspiration" has almost as many meanings as there are denominations. "Salvation" slams shut many mental doors and opens an equal number of emotional flood-gates. Some preachers grasp a word like "existential" and use it without knowing what it really means.

Or on another level, people often feel compelled to label or categorize every preacher heard or every author read. It is easy to call a man a personalist, a liberal, a naturalist, a neo-orthodox, or a fundamentalist and then write him off as unacceptable or as a new prophet, depending upon the emotional reaction to that particular label. Such labeling is a substitute for appraisal. Having conveniently pigeonholed a man or an idea, one needs no longer grapple with the elements of truth embedded in the thought.

Since words are the most common basis for good communication, and are also symbols, it is true in a sense that most speaking and writing are done by means of labels. The problem is to select the labels (symbols-words) not supercharged with emotional connotations and overloaded with symbolism. A preacher needs to be certain that everyone knows the meaning of every word he uses—including the preacher himself. If there is a possibility of misinterpretation he should establish his use of every important term. He also has a responsibility to be sure he correctly understands and interprets the thinking of any individual or school of thought which he presumes to label.

In controversial areas it is well to remember that a man is

not a position, a point of view; he is a person. He must be understood as a whole being. On this basis there is fellowship even in disagreement and the participants in a discussion can relish their varying views. It is particularly important in religion that the lines of communication be kept open. The preacher who would preserve his own integrity and still be persuasive needs to understand the power of words and be willing to discipline himself to a close scrutiny of his use of language.

Unfortunately, some preachers do not take the matter of language seriously, particularly on the level of proper usage. Many offend because of misuse of English. The preacher who begins his sermon by saying "The other day I come upon a book . . ." may find his congregation coming upon more interesting considerations—even to counting the panes in the stained-glass windows. A "between you and I" may come between the congregation and the Gospel. The preacher is not in the pulpit to please every pedantic English teacher who pounces upon superfluous present participles as if they were fleas, but while he is in the pulpit he needs to command the respect of the members of his congregation even to the use of good English. Such care may call for a dictionary at the side of his Bible and a thesaurus next to St. Augustine.

Self-improvement may begin by looking up all new words he discovers in his reading, then easing them into use. An evening with excellent prose, such as the speeches of Winston Churchill, does wonders for any public speaker. If in addition to all the efforts a preacher can exert by himself, he then has a kindly critic who can help him separate the chaff from the wheat in his style, he may thank God and take courage. These concerns are not too much to ask of a man whose message depends on the use of words as vehicles of truth.

The proper use of language is to clarify thought, not to mystify an audience. ". . . If you in a tongue utter speech that is not intelligible, how will anyone know what is said? For you will be speaking into the air," said Paul. If language is to be clear it must be specific, for only specific words have power to cut into the imagination—to make others feel, hear, see, taste. Whenever an idea lends itself to visualization it should be presented in such manner as to call up exact images in the listeners' minds—images that have size, shape, color, movement. Since people think in images—"with pictures in their heads"—the preacher's task is to use language which makes his ideas come to life at once.

Ministers are often rightly accused of being abstract, vague, the possessors of a vocabulary marked by theological jargon and multimeaninged words. Take a look at, or better still, make a list of the words constantly used to express elements in the Christian faith: sin, grace, love, holiness, God, atonement, heaven, kingdom, hell, forgiveness, evil, glory, tolerance, and faith. Occasionally one hears rumblings that these words should be discarded and others substituted but such a substitution would not solve the problem of understanding the ideas involved. "Right living" might be used for "righteousness," but this change overlooks the added Biblical dimension that righteousness is also part of salvation itself. Or "faith," a word which is in the daily vocabulary, is commonly used to mean belief or intellectual assent. In Paul's thinking this interpretation would be quite inadequate. He saw faith as a total involvement of mind, emotions, and will. Rather than changing the theological vocabulary the preacher would do well to understand the concept and then present it in words and pictures which can be grasped by the congregation.

The preacher is indeed dealing with a difficult assignment. Of necessity, he is talking about intangibles, doctrines, spiritual values. It is not easy always to make these concepts live. Yet, his task is to be concrete, concise, and vivid in order to give these ideas flesh and blood.

Van Loon's writings are full of the picturesque phrases. For example:

High up in the North in the land called Svithjod, there stands a rock. It is a hundred miles high and a hundred miles wide. Once every thousand years a little bird comes to this rock to sharpen its beak.

When the rock has thus been worn away, then a single day of eternity will have gone by.

This fantasy may not be the theologian's last word on eternity but it is an apt expression of an abstract concept couched in suggestive and exciting language. Would that the preacher could "go thou and do likewise" with many of the abstract terms in which he lives, moves, and has his being.

Or again, no one has ordained E. B. White, yet this expert writer for the *New Yorker* should have a long apostolic succession of ministers seeking to do what he does with language.

We received a letter from the Writers' War Board the other day asking for a statement on "The Meaning of Democracy." It presumably is our duty to comply with such a request, and it is certainly our pleasure.

Surely the Board knows what democracy is. It is the line that forms on the right. It is the don't in Don't Shove. It is the hole in the stuffed shirt through which the sawdust slowly trickles; it is the dent in the high hat. Democracy is the recurrent suspicion that more than half of the people are right more than half of the time. It is the feeling of privacy in the voting booths, the feeling of communion in the libraries, the feeling of vitality everywhere. Democracy is the score at the beginning of the ninth. It is an idea which hasn't been disproved yet, a song the words of which have not gone bad. It's the mustard on the hot dog and the cream in the rationed coffee. Democracy is a request from the War Board, in the middle of a morning in the middle of a war, wanting to know what democracy is.[2]

Here is a thoughtful attempt to take a multimeaninged word, "democracy," and give it some life, put it in a picturesque scene which captures the imagination.

Examination of examples of vivid writing discloses several characteristics of good word use—good language for preaching. The first requirement is that the language shall be accurate; that specific words be used instead of general ones. For example, "He went down the street." "Went" could profitably be replaced by marched, sauntered, shuffled, staggered, or swaggered. One of these verbs relays to the listeners exactly what the preacher is trying to portray. Or, "Jesus set his face steadfastly to go to Jeruaslem." A sermon could open up on the manner and attitude Jesus showed toward that eventful journey. One specific word, "steadfastly," vivifies what the chronicler was trying to portray.

[2] E. B. White, *The Wild Flag*, Boston, Houghton, 1946, p. 31.

Accuracy of language depends upon clarity of thought. When C. S. Lewis wanted to show the nature of theology, he recognized the point of view of the hard-bitten old officer who said he had no use for theology, but that he had felt God out alone in the desert at night. Lewis then goes on:

Now in a sense I quite agreed with that man. I think he'd probably had a real experience of God in the desert. And when he turned from that experience to the Christian creeds, I think he *was* really turning from something quite real to something less real. In the same way, if a man has once looked at the Atlantic from the beach, and then goes and looks at a map of the Atlantic, he also will be turning from something more real to something less real: turning from real waves to a bit of coloured paper. But here comes the point. The map *is* only coloured paper, but there are two things you have to remember about it. In the first place, it is based on what hundreds and thousands of people have found out by sailing the real Atlantic. In that way it has behind it masses of experience just as real as the one you could have from the beach; only, while yours would be a single isolated glimpse, the map fits all those different experiences together. In the second place, if you want to go anywhere, the map is absolutely necessary. As long as you're content with walks on the beach, your own glimpses are far more fun than looking at a map. But the map's going to be more use than walks on the beach if you want to get to America.

Well, Theology's like the map . . .[3]

Simplicity is another characteristic of effective style in speaking or writing. Force is related to simplicity, for force is often achieved when there is an economy of language and the words are short and specific. If force is difficult to describe, its antithesis is not. Many preachers use long and awkward sentences, too many adjectives, polysyllabic words, and redundant phrases. A preacher's style improves when he uses simple sentences, short Anglo-Saxon words, and strong verbs.

Lest someone think that simplicity vitiates emotional force in writing or speech, listen to these words of Winston Churchill spoken immediately after the British defeat at Dunkerque:

We shall defend our island, whatever the cost may be. We shall fight on the beaches. We shall fight on the landing grounds. We

[3] C. S. Lewis, *Beyond Personality*, New York, Macmillan, 1945, pp. 1-2.

shall fight in the fields and in the streets, and we shall fight in the hills. We shall never surrender.

Suggestiveness is another characteristic of good usage. Suggestiveness is simply the use of words and concepts that stir up imaginations. Some words have rich connotations beyond the actual dictionary meaning. Compare, for example, the words house and home; woman and mother; First Cause and God. In a funeral service, phrases like "The Lord is my Shepherd," "In My Father's house are many mansions," and "God is my refuge and strength" have meaningful connotations for the bereaved because they are freighted with suggestion.

One of the important aspects of the parables of Jesus is the imaginative language which suggests so much more than the parables actually say—the sower and the seed, the lost coin, the prodigal son, and the rich young ruler. All of these words have meaning, but they are rich also in the imaginative quality which adds much to the receptivity of the ideas themselves.

For a modern example, take the words of Herbert Butterfield speaking of the action of God in history. He remarks that instead of picturing God as a heavy hand interposed to interfere with a heavy piece of machinery (the world), it would be better to picture "a child who played her piece very badly when she was alone, but when the music teacher sat at her side played it passably well, though the music teacher never touched her, never said anything, but operated by pure sympathetic attraction and by just being there."[4] Such a description not only dramatizes the idea, but uses language imaginatively so that people are able to grasp the full meaning of the idea behind the illustration.

Good style is also characterized by ease, by the use of language that is natural and unobtrusive, by informal structure. This does not mean the use of slang, cant or specialized jargon excepting in rare cases, but it does call for sensory language and a conversational style on a high level. The development of this ease helps bridge the gap which many preachers feel

[4] Herbert Butterfield, *Christianity and History*, London, G. Bell, 1949, p. iii.

between their written and their spoken styles. If a preacher finds that when he writes he labors overmuch on polished language and balanced sentences, he should work more on a spoken style which will give the ring of "honest talk." On the other hand, if the preacher speaks with cat-and-dog sentences, is ungrammatical and repetitive, then he should probably spend more time writing. Fortunate the preacher who is so natural in his writing and speaking that both styles reflected the same personality.

Because ease is associated with simplicity it should not be thought that ease detracts from beauty or the use if imagery. Read aloud the 23rd Psalm as an example of ease combined with beauty, or take these words from Lincoln's Second Inaugural Address:

> With malice toward none; with charity for all; with firmness in the right, as God gives us to see the right, let us strive on to finish the work we are in; to bind up the nation's wounds; to care for him who shall have borne the battle, and for his widow, and his orphan —to do all which may achieve and cherish a just and lasting peace among ourselves, and with all nations.

Although the mastery of grammar and rhetoric may not be the most glamorous task in the world it becomes important when recognized as part of a preacher's equipment for persuasive preaching. If he is dedicated to the Gospel, he is equally dedicated to the best means of expressing that message.

CHAPTER VIII

DELIVERY AS PERSUASION

SEMINARY students often assume that after their "call" they can concentrate on their theology and that they will somehow be automatically endowed with the attributes of effective delivery. The Seminaries themselves have been somewhat guilty in fostering this attitude for they have followed the practice of teaching what to say is in one course and how to say it in another. One teacher of preachers went still farther when he declared that as long as a student had something to say he did not care how it was said.

A preacher who desires to be persuasive in his preaching has to recognize the fact that people listen to a sermon as a whole. They are affected by its content, structure, illustrations, and delivery. Therefore the preacher needs to be concerned with the total impact of the sermon—including its delivery. The ineffectiveness of many sermons illustrates the indissoluble relationship between content and delivery. Lack of fervor in delivery is often the result of a trivial idea or the absence of clear structure. Again, a poor voice or slovenly enunciation blunts the cutting edge of a well-structured sermon. The preacher needs to have all his tools sharp.

There are several reasons why seminary students resist assiduous work on delivery. Many of them go into the ministry because they have a natural aptitude for standing on their feet and talking; therefore they feel secure in their manner of delivery. Others come to the seminary after preaching throughout part of their college years and their amateur pattern of delivery is unfortunately already set. Some do not take kindly to criticism, while others think of the seminary as highly professional training and delivery as college stuff.

Yet, there are examples on every hand to prove that the most persuasive preachers are those who are effective in delivery. Moreover, most of them have worked on their delivery with as much determination as they have labored over the other aspects of their sermonizing. One of the most competent preachers in the Presbyterian Church once said that while in seminary he spent five or ten minutes a day in the preaching laboratory verbalizing—anything that came to his mind so that he could get into the habit of having words respond to his command. In this way he developed a facility of speech. An outstanding Methodist bishop hides himself away before delivering any sermon to verbalize his speech once or twice. Another prominent minister returned to his seminary for a summer because he said he had neglected delivery as a student and now found it was his greatest problem. Granted that occasionally a preacher may be good in delivery and have nothing to say, by and large the most persuasive speaker will be effective because of the total impact of ideas, structure, personality, and delivery.

Probably every member of a congregation would agree that it is to a preacher's advantage to hold himself erect, to walk with confidence, and to stand on his own two feet when preaching. Many preachers, however, find the pulpit stand a "refuge and strength, a very present help in time of trouble," and hold onto it as if their stance were in jeopardy. Equally distressing is the black-gowned preacher with arms outstretched for long intervals as if he were the Bat-man about to take off. The preacher who has the wanderlust during his sermons also begets uneasiness on the part of his congregation, especially if his pacing is the result of uncontrolled nervous energy. If he cannot curtail his ramblings he can at least provide himself with a boxlike pulpit that helps set a boundary to his peregrinations.

In a consideration of gestures in delivery a line from the

musical, *Annie Get Your Gun,* provides a good text: "Doin' what comes natur'lly." Happily, the day of teaching specific gestures for specific moods is past. But the need for gestures remains. The easiest dictum is that mood and message dictate action; and that the action should not distract the audience's attention from the idea. Generally the problems of gesturing do not come from the abundance of action, but from a lack of it. Many preachers stand in their pulpits like wooden Indians. Whatever the cause of this stiffness—natural reserve, desire for dignity, studied control of overgesturing—it is not normal behavior. A man who has good news to share usually portrays his feelings with spontaneous reactions. The preacher proclaims the greatest Good News the world has ever heard and it is inconceivable that he can discuss it with no bodily reaction. He need not flail his arms like a windmill but the intensity of the idea within him will at times necessitate more than a vocal outlet.

Facial expression is important in the effective delivery of a sermon. Unconsciously a preacher's face gives clues to the congregation which either support or counteract the words he is saying. When a preacher speaks of Christian love, his face reflects whether he is talking from theory or experience. It is sad for any preacher to let a good face go to waste in the pulpit. However, like gestures, facial expressions at times need to be curbed. One young preacher had a most infectious smile which reflected a warm, friendly personality. Even when he enunciated some hard saying of the Gospel he unconsciously broke into his smile. The effect was not what he would have wanted had he been able to see himself. In practice sessions, the use of a mirror helps many public speakers. Facial expressions and gestures both may be carefully studied, if the speaker will forget his self-consciousness when he again steps into the pulpit.

There is a dramatic quality about an occasional glance away from the congregation, but as a regular procedure an audience does not care to have the preacher gaze at the ceiling, look longingly out the window, or bury his head in his notes. *The Rime of the Ancient Mariner* has a delightful line: "He holds them with his glittering eye . . ." So may the preacher's eye glitter with concern for recognition of his message. No preacher wants to sweep the congregation row upon row but he can encompass the group by directing his eyes at people as if he were genuinely interested in conversing with them.

Not every preacher is gifted with a good voice, but if he recognizes persuasive power of the voice, every preacher can strive to develop his own to its highest potential. The most important aspects of voice are timbre, force, melody, resonance, and articulation. In an endeavor to overthrow the old abuses of elocution other matters have been emphasized, sometimes to the detriment of the use of the voice. The world's future does not hang on diaphragmatic breathing, but a careful preacher should know how to breathe when speaking, for correct breathing goes a long way in determining the quality of the voice as well as providing energy needed to sustain the voice. A good voice or a speech teacher can give the conscientious preacher some tips on the use of the voice. Also a preacher can get into the habit of listening to the quality of his own voice. The least he can do is to open his mouth wide and read slowly, taking a deep breath before he begins. That alone would help the quality of many a preacher's voice.

Force is another important factor in the use of the voice. An amazing number of preachers cannot project their voices; they have no force. Perhaps this is due to the advent of the "conversational style." Many preachers talk as if they were in a phone booth afraid of being overheard by an F.B.I. agent. Rather than correct this gross sin in speaking, they add a loud speaker to the sanctuary. It is appalling to see the number of small churches which have a mechanical speaker to help the preacher project his voice to the back row. If a public address system is not one of the seven deadly sins, it is surely a close eighth, for even the best loud speaker gives the natural voice a metallic ring and enables the preacher to get by with a slovenly delivery. George Whitefield, who could speak to ten thousand in an out-of-doors setting, would be shocked at his ministerial progeny if he could hear them whispering into an amplified speaker. Reading aloud is an excellent way to increase forcefulness. The preacher who has difficulty in projecting his voice could improve if he entered the pulpit on a Saturday evening, took a long passage of Scripture and read as if he wanted a partially deaf man on the back row to hear it. This does not necessitate shouting; but it should mean deep-breathing, an open mouth, good articulation, and some conscious effort put into making each syllable of every word carry its own weight. It is too much to ask an audience to go to church and work every minute to hear what the preacher has to say.

Force is related to fervor. Some sermons have the spark of a load of wet cement. The preacher may be talking about the most important thing in the world and yet deliver his sermon as if he were casually reciting the names and addresses in a telephone book. He cannot be persuasive if he is not alive physically, if he is not inwardly excited about what he has to say. How can one talk dispassionately about the Good News in Christ? The preacher who believes he has something important to impart, that his message is something his congregation needs to hear, that he is well prepared—that preacher will speak with fervor. He will be convincing. Now it is easier to have fervor for something specific than for a vague, abstract idea. A man speaks with natural warmth about experiences he has lived through, situations he has witnessed, problems that have perplexed him. Thoreau, once commented, "I would not talk about myself so much if there were anyone else I knew as well."

A good voice is a melodious voice, with variation and range. Two typical pulpit diseases are the monotone and the ministerial melody. The monotone kills the sermon and paralyzes the congregation. The ministerial melody—that supersanctimonious rising and falling of the voice—produces a weaving effect in the minds of the hearers which leaves them half dizzy. Both of these diseases are relatively easy to cure. The monotone needs to convince himself that his material is important and alive. Then he needs to sprinkle his sermons liberally with illustrations told as he would expect to describe them if he were witnessing them, so that he will have to change pace as he emphasizes the meaning he is trying to convey. Reading aloud, vocalizing a sermon, and listening for the good tones in the voice will all help break the habit of monotonous speech.

There are also several cures open to the preacher with the ministerial tone. He can record his voice and study it. He can repeatedly ask himself, "Do I sound like a real person talking to real people?" If his sermon reflects the kinds of rhythms and sounds he would not use in the grocery store, then he needs remedial work. By reading prose materials out loud—the newspaper, news articles, editorials—he will begin to feel the natural speech rhythms which can be used in the pulpit as well as in daily conversation. If he has the courage, he will enlist his wife and his children to take him apart when he lapses from a human being into a preacher! It is the tone quality and the rhythms of everyday usage that are under consideration, not the word forms. Casual conversation is full of contractions, fragmentary sentences, provincialisms, and slang. Such speech is not the speech of the pulpit.

A proper rate of speaking causes some preachers difficulty. An occasional preacher talks so slowly, weighing every word, that the congregation becomes impatient. Just as a good pitcher does not throw the same pitch all the time, so the preacher should be wary of plodding along at the same rate. If he has a natural tendency to speak too slowly he may help himself by becoming better acquainted with his material before going into the pulpit; he can lighten it up with illustrations; he can follow his notes a little more closely. One preacher when criticized for his slow speech replied that he wanted the congregation to get the feeling that he was actually thinking about what he was saying. However, exactly the reverse reaction was taking place—the congregation wished he would do his thinking before he came into the pulpit. On the other hand, if a preacher speaks too fast the chances are that he does not enunciate clearly and cannot be easily understood. The saving factor in rapid speaking is the pause so that the speaker can get his breath and the audience can catch up with his thinking. Often in so-called fast speaking the rate is not the fault as much as the unbroken flow. The preacher who speaks rapidly, even if clearly, needs to practice a change of pace as surely as does his tortoise brother.

Timbre or resonance is the quality which gives pleasantness and fullness to the voice. Proper breathing, a willingness to open the mouth, and practice in reading out loud can do much to improve voice timbre. Any nasal defect which impairs the voice should have the attention of a specialist.

The last important factor of a good voice is articulation. Many preachers are slovenly in enunciating words. They say "govment," "howjado," "kep'," "comin'." Articulation of this kind makes a sensitive listener wince and it also destroys the force of the thought behind the words. If all other qualities of a good voice are denied a preacher, this one is of his own making. He can read, read, read aloud and with each reading resolve: "I will enunciate each syllable of each word clearly before I leave it, if it takes all day to read one psalm." This will force him to open his mouth wide, to strengthen his tongue and jaw muscles, and to use his teeth more effectively. He may begin by reading the 46th Psalm:

God is our re - fuge and streng - th, a ver - y pre - sent help in trouble.

After a few verses he may find that he is no longer sliding over his words without giving all the syllables the respect due them. In addition to exercises, a visit to a radio station to watch an announcer read a commercial is recommended. He may see the announcer contort his face and screw up his mouth, but he will hear each word come out distinctly and without error.

There is much discussion of the relative merits of the written sermon, the memorized sermon and the extemporaneous sermon. Doubtless there is another category into which many sermons would fall—the impromptu. But the sin of impromptu preaching is so gross that it should not be recognized as a type. There are advantages to each type of sermon delivery. If a sermon is memorized, the preacher is forced to write out his material and writing tends to make for exactness, good style, clarity of idea, and usually for succinctness. Memorization also enables him to dispense with notes except as he may need a few "jottings" as reminders of paragraph headings. Thus he is able to look at his congregation, which gives a directness to his delivery.

In spite of these apparent values, most preachers are aware of the pitfalls of memorizing. For one thing, it takes an inordinate amount of time to commit to memory eight or ten pages of material. Also it tends to put emphasis upon style and particular words and to minimize ideas. Further, memorization tends to place the speaker in a strait jacket; he must concentrate on words on a paper back in his study, and new ideas and illustrations seldom come to him on his feet. As a result, intruding circumstances may upset him because his concentration must be intense. Perhaps the greatest fault of memorizing, however, is that it destroys the spontaneity associated with fervent speaking. A preacher who memorizes is likely to be so conscious of style and language that he finds it impossible to be persuasive.

Occasionally a preacher will declare that he memorizes because he cannot think on his feet. No doubt if a person absolutely cannot think on his feet, and yet desires to look at his congregation, then memorization may be the only way out. However, before he spends the time involved in memorizing, he might remember that everyone can learn to speak in a manner which will allow him more freedom to think as he speaks.

In many ways the easiest method of delivering a sermon is to write it out and read it. The reading method has all of the advantages to the preacher of writing out the manuscript for memorization with the added asset of having the material in front of him as he preaches. However, a manuscript often takes away both the spontaneity and the directness of delivery so necessary in persuasive preaching. The ordinary preacher, unless he has a strong outline under the sermon, is likely to read a literary essay on "Patience," "Humility," or "Christian Love." An audience does not like to be read to for thirty minutes, unless it is listening to Charles Laughton giving a reading performance. But the preacher is not giving a performance. Aside from the fact that a written manuscript is often too literary, the person-to-person impact so necessary to persuasive speaking is sacrificed. Occasionally a student in practice preaching contends that the congregation does not know he has a manuscript. One is always tempted to ask the young man if he preaches to a blind congregation. The average preacher who takes a manuscript into the pulpit looks at his notes more than he thinks he does, and is usually mentally indirect, particularly because his written style is more literary than his spoken style. Of course, it can be pointed out that some of the pulpit "greats" do take manuscripts into the pulpit. The only thing to be said in answer is that there are exceptions and that these exceptions usually spend an extraordinary amount of time in sermon preparation. The preacher who sits down and writes out a sermon which he does not mentally assimilate, then reads it from the pulpit on Sunday morning, can hardly expect to be a "great" exception—nor a persuasive speaker.

The extemporaneous method is probably the most persuasive way to deliver a sermon. Frequently impromptu speaking is confused with extemporaneous speaking. A tremendous amount of preparation is needed for a good extemporaneous talk, and brief notes may also be used by the speaker. The steps in sermon preparation—the thesis, outline, purpose, response sought—all must be written out and clearly thought through. The wording must then be considered. Following this, the preacher needs to verbalize the sermon several times to know whether his ideas are properly expressed.

The great reluctance to rely on extemporaneous speaking comes from those who stop short of this last step in preparation. Students often say, "I keep getting tied up in my sentences, back out, repeat myself, and labor the point. My style is awful." Or they say, "I split infinitives and dangle participles all over the pulpit. In general, I feel as if I just grope around." It is true that in the beginning the extemporaneous preacher may perhaps have to sacrifice style. Yet, his rapport with his congregation and the earnestness he achieves because of his freedom usually compensate for these faults. Besides, as he becomes more accustomed to this method of preaching, he will find that he begins to fashion good sentences on his feet, that his grammar and style improve, and that above all he is keeping the spontaneity, directness, and freedom so necessary to persuasive preaching.

Sometimes a preacher may use a combination of writing and

verbalizing in the extemporaneous method. After he has the outline he may verbalize some portions as well as write out some passages. Many preachers write out their introductions and conclusions as well as the transitions between points.

Extemporaneous speakers differ in their use of notes. A few key phrases should be enough to remind a preacher of the points in his outline. If notes are used the best method is to type them, or write them large enough to be easily read, on large cards. Notes are nothing to be ashamed of. They should not be crammed onto small scraps of paper nor slipped surreptitiously into the hymnal or Bible.

If the list of considerations for good delivery seems long the rewards for their mastery are equally impressive: a favorably disposed audience, a warm response, and lives committed to the Gospel.

The preacher who is dedicated to the task of preaching because he believes in the Gospel can say with the writer of II Timothy: "I know whom I have believed." Or with St. Paul: "For I am not ashamed of the gospel." Recognizing his commitment, he need not hesitate in witnessing to and proclaiming the Word of God as long as he relates it to the people who sit before him.

Finally, the preacher who desires to be persuasive has a good model in St. Paul who said he became all things to all men that he might be the means of saving some. For Paul this did not mean that the nature of the Gospel was changed to suit the occasion, but the means of presenting it were adjusted to deal with the different groups whom he faced: slaves, kings, Jews, Gentiles. The modern preacher, too, is called upon to adapt his message to those whom he faces in as persuasive a way as possible. With St. Paul his motivation can be these ringing words: "I do it all for the sake of the Gospel, that I may share in its blessings."